# simply handmade

# 365 easy gifts & decorations you can make

Meredith® Press
An imprint of Meredith® Books

Meredith® Press
An imprint of Meredith® Books

# Simply Handmade: 365 Easy Gifts & Decorations You Can Make

Editor: Carol Field Dahlstrom
Technical Editor: Susan Banker
Graphic Designer: Marisa Dirks
Copy Chief: Catherine Hamrick
Copy and Production Editor: Terri Fredrickson
Contributing Copy Editor: Jill Philby
Contributing Proofreader: Colleen Johnson
Electronic Production Coordinator: Paula Forest
Editorial and Design Assistants: Judy Bailey, Treesa Landry, Karen Schirm
Production Director: Douglas M. Johnston
Production Manager: Pam Kvitne
Assistant Prepress Manager: Marjorie J. Schenkelberg

**Meredith® Books**
Editor in Chief: James D. Blume
Design Director: Matt Strelecki
Managing Editor: Gregory H. Kayko

Director, Sales & Marketing, Retail: Michael A. Peterson
Director, Sales & Marketing, Special Markets: Rita McMullen
Director, Sales & Marketing, Home & Garden Center Channel: Ray Wolf
Director, Operations: George A. Susral

Vice President, General Manager: Jamie L. Martin

**Meredith Publishing Group**
President, Publishing Group: Christopher M. Little
Vice President, Consumer Marketing & Development: Hal Oringer

**Meredith Corporation**
Chairman and Chief Executive Officer: William T. Kerr

Chairman of the Executive Committee: E. T. Meredith III

All of us at Meredith® Press are dedicated to providing you with information and ideas to enhance your home. We welcome your comments and suggestions. Write to us at: Meredith® Press, Crafts Department, 1716 Locust St., Des Moines, IA 50309-3023.

**Cover photography:** Andy Lyons
**Cover projects:** Jeweled Christmas Balls, pages 52–53; Sparkling Beaded Candleholder, page 54
**Back cover projects:** Goblet Centerpiece, pages 112–113; Autumn Harvest Place Cards, pages 14–15; Keepsake Rose Heart, pages 100–101
**Inside front cover projects:** Beaded Bobesche, page 151; Simply Stunning Pumpkin, page 13; Winter Wool Snowflake, pages 102–103
**Inside back cover projects:** Summertime Bow, pages 202–203; Frosted Ornament Trim, pages 68–69; Jelly Bean Pots, pages 174–175

# simply handmade

The joy of creating gifts and decorations is enhanced when we see them bring happiness to those around us. When we make objects to share with others or to decorate our homes, we feel an extra sense of pride and satisfaction.

Every day of the year brings a reason to celebrate and each season lends itself to holidays and times for sharing handmade items. We've filled this book with more than 365 ideas for you to try and provided tips and techniques to suit each special time of the year.

Creating wonderful gifts and decorations need not take a lot of time. All of the projects in this book can be done quickly—usually in an evening. But the satisfaction you receive from making them will last a lifetime. We hope that the projects you create using the ideas in this book will please you and your family and friends all year long.

*Carol Field Dahlstrom*

# about this book...

In this book you'll find delightful projects to make for each season of the year. There are gifts to create and give, and fun projects to make and use in decorating your home. Nearly all of the ideas in this book can be done in an evening and you need not be an experienced crafter to make them. To help you decide which ones to try first, we've divided the projects into three kinds:

## If your guests are at the door...

look for our *Good Ideas* projects. They take little time to make with materials you have on hand.

## If you have just a little time...

to create something, look for our *Make It In Minutes* projects. These ideas require a few more materials but are simple to do.

## If you want to try a new and easy technique... look for our *Step-by-Step*

projects that are quick to make but will introduce you to a new technique or material with step-by-step photographs and instructions.

By making gifts and decorations all year-round, you'll experience the joy of creating and telling your family and friends, "I made it myself."

# contents

## fall
*pages 6–49*

Celebrate autumn with creative accents you can make, even if you have only minutes to spare. From clever candles to pumpkins that range from whimsical to elegant, these ideas will inspire you to create an unforgettable autumn season for your whole family.

## winter
*pages 50–131*

When the days turn frosty and the joyous holiday spirit begins to fill your heart, what better time to make handcrafted treasures to trim your home and share with loved ones. This festive collection will add a merry note all winter long.

## spring
*pages 132–177*

You'll be busy this spring perfecting favorite techniques like etching, beading, and mosaics. While the assortment of fun projects seems to require intricate skills, they're actually easy to complete.

## summer
*pages 178–213*

Bring the beauty of summer indoors with ideas that will brighten even a cloudy day. All of these delightful projects are quick to make, so you can enjoy creating gifts and decorations without missing any of summer's sunshine.

*The future belongs to those who believe
in the beauty of their dreams.*

—— ELEANOR ROOSEVELT

The crisp days of autumn inspire the cocooning in all of us as we settle in for cooler days to come. Celebrate this glorious season by creating projects rich in color and texture to give away or to decorate your home.

fall

# golden
## autumn
### leaves

# Make these elegant leaves in an evening

using nature's patterns from real leaves, window screen, and a little sparkle of paint.

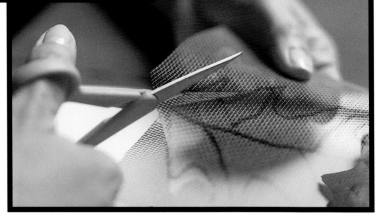

**1** **Collect your favorite fall leaves.** Pick shapes that have some cleanly formed edges. Cut the window screen a little larger than the leaf. Lay the screen on some newspaper and spray the screen gold. Let it dry and paint it on the other side. Let the paint dry thoroughly.

**2** **Lay the leaf** on a piece of white paper and put the painted window screen over the leaf. Draw around the leaf with the permanent marker. Add the veins of the leaf with marker.

**Cut out the leaf** using old scissors. **3**

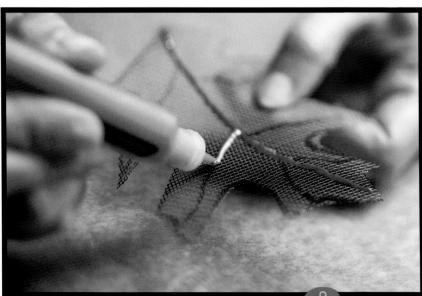

**4** **Using the paint pen,** draw around the leaf and add the veins. Let the paint dry. Bend the leaf slightly to make it look real.

**To make the leaves you will need:**
Real leaves (oak and maple leaves have wonderful shapes)
Window screen (available by the foot at hardware stores)
Newspaper
Gold spray paint
White typing paper
Permanent black marker
Old scissors
Gold, copper, or bronze paint pen (often used for fabric painting—available at fabric, discount, and craft stores)

## 1 more idea...
● Scatter the graceful leaves about a real pumpkin trimmed with gold stripes, and you have created a centerpiece to celebrate the season.

## also try this...
● Share your leaf gathering for this project with your children. They'll enjoy learning about the different shapes of leaves and types of trees.

# vintage button wreath

Grandma's button box holds the key to this clever wreath that can be completed in a snap.

**To make the wreath you will need:**

Vintage and/or new buttons in various sizes and desired colors

Assorted buckles

Hot-glue gun and hot-glue sticks

Grapevine wreath in desired size

## 2 more ideas...

- Spray paint the grapevine wreath white and then accent with bright colored buttons for a more contemporary look.

- For other fun-to-make wreaths, replace the buttons with old game pieces, jewelry, or wrapped candies.

**here's how** **To make this project** glue a few buttons and buckles together to make small groupings. Arrange and glue these groupings to the grapevine wreath. Add single buttons between groupings as desired.

# country topiaries

A simple raffia bow is the finishing touch
on these oh-so-easy tabletop topiaries.

**To make the topiary you will need:**
4-inch terra-cotta pot
Styrofoam® piece
    to fit in pot
Wooden dowel or
    small tree branch
Miniature pumpkin
Hot-glue gun and
    hot-glue sticks
Dried beans or peas
Raffia

**here's how** **To make this project** glue the Styrofoam into the pot. Sharpen the end of the dowel or branch (trimming it to size if necessary). Push it into the bottom of the pumpkin. Push the other end of the dowel into the Styrofoam. Hot-glue the dowel to secure if necessary. Spread dried beans or peas over the top of the Styrofoam, gluing if desired. Using raffia, tie a bow around the dowel just below the pumpkin.

## 2 more ideas...

● For other interesting tabletop topiaries, replace the miniature pumpkins with small gourds.

● If you want your topiary to last for more than two weeks, use artificial vegetables or fruits.

# good ideas *simply stunning pumpkins*

**Embellish small pumpkins** and interestingly shaped gourds with a simple ribbon bow or a dusting of metallic gold paint. For a fun display indoors or out, stack carved pumpkins and add a swirl of gold-bead garland for a one-of-a-kind jack-o'-lantern totem pole.

# autumn harvest place cards

Welcome guests to the table with these personalized autumn bouquets, surprisingly tucked into textured waffle cones.

**To make a place card you will need:**
Clear acrylic spray
Giant waffle cone for ice cream
Fiberfill
Hot-glue gun and hot-glue sticks
Preserved leaves, berries, and wheat
Gold glitter paint pen (often used for fabric painting— available at fabric, discount, and craft stores)
18 inches of gold ribbon
String

**here's how** **To make this project** spray the cone with three or four coats of acrylic spray. Push a handful of fiberfill down into the bottom of the cone. Hot-glue the leaves and fruit into the opening of the cone, beginning with the large leaves and then adding berries, wheat, and smaller leaves. Use the glitter paint pen to write a person's name at one end of the ribbon and allow it to dry. Fold the ribbon in half and tie a piece of string around the ribbon approximately 1½ inches down from the fold to make a loop. Glue ribbon, under the loop, to the top of the cone. Cover the string tie with smaller leaves and berries.

## 2 more ideas...
● For an edible version of this project, don't use acrylic spray and fill the cone with nuts and candies.

● Use this ribbon idea to add a personalized message to any gift.

# good ideas *silly popcorn treats*

## The kids will love these ghoulish treats!

Just whip up a batch of popcorn balls (corn syrup in the recipe helps to make the fun surprises stick—see the recipe on *page 216*) then add in a few gummy worms, black licorice bits, candy corn, or other candies in Halloween colors.

# colorful necktie garland

Cut in the shape of a necktie tip. you can create a **clever garland** using your **favorite fabric scraps.**

**To make the garland you will need:**
A necktie to use as the pattern
Various fabric scraps
Sewing thread
Pearl beads

**here's how** **To make this project** use the end of a necktie for the pattern. Use the pattern to cut shapes from fabrics (two for each print), adding ¼-inch seams. Sew the shapes together in pairs, with right sides facing, leaving the top edges open. Trim the points, turn, and press. Press under the top seam and sew closed. Add a pearl to each tip. Stitch the shapes together at the top corners.

## 1 more idea...
● Use these unique garlands as edgings for shelves or trims on curtains, tablecloths, or table runners.

## also try this...
● Replace the pearl with a jingle bell to make a festive Christmastime garland for the mantel.

# wrapped up Halloween goodies

Wrap candies in a pair of tulle circles

and tie up tight for

special treat bundles

to give to favorite little

ghouls and

goblins.

**here's how** **To make this project** cut 8-inch circles out of tulle. Using two circles, lay one atop the other. Place a handful of candy in the center of the fabric. Gather the fabric up over the candy and tie with a ribbon bow or twist with a pipe cleaner to secure. To make spiral ends on the pipecleaner, simply wind the ends around a pencil or dowel.

## 2 more ideas...

- For those special little trick-or-treaters, add a plastic spider ring or wiggly eyes to the pipecleaner tie.

- Fill these elegant bags with mints and nuts for an upcoming wedding or tea.

23

# nature's beauty centerpiece

**To make the pinecone balls you will need:**
Styrofoam balls in desired sizes
Brown acrylic spray paint
Small pinecones or leaves
Hot-glue gun and hot-glue sticks

## 2 more ideas...

• Use a topiary shaped piece of pre-formed Styrofoam (available in craft stores) as the base for an interesting autumn centerpiece.

• Incorporate other fall findings (acorns, small twig slices, etc.) to add a variety of colors and textures to your spheres.

A walk in the woods—or even your backyard—

is all it takes to gather the findings for these

autumn-time treasures.

**here's how** **To make this project** spray-paint the Stryofoam ball with brown paint and let it dry completely. Glue the stem end of the pinecones, or the front of the leaves, to the ball wedging or overlapping them together so the ball does not show. Keep adding pinecones or leaves until the Stryrofoam ball is completely covered.

# copper and brass napkin rings

Free-formed wire rings hold
**glistening beads and buttons**
to create designer-look jewelry
for cloth dinner napkins.

**To make the
napkin rings
you will need:**

Spool of 16-gauge
brass wire (wires
are available at
hardware stores)
Spool of 18-gauge
copper wire
Paper towel or
toilet paper tube
Wire cutters
Needle-nose pliers
A variety of beads
or buttons
Fine spool wire

**here's how** **To make this project** bend a small hook at the end of the brass wire. Wrap it around the paper tube seven to nine times, crisscrossing it upon itself. Cut the wire off the spool, allowing enough wire to bend around to meet the first end. Bend a hook at the end and connect the two ends together. Use pliers to pinch the ends together and remove from the tube.

Cut a 30-inch length of copper wire and secure the end to the outside edge of the brass wire. If using beads, string them onto the copper wire and adjust them as you wrap the brass wire. To keep the beads from falling off the wire while wrapping, bend a hook in the wire. Secure the end to the outside edge of brass wire, snipping off any extra wire. Attach buttons to the ring by tying them on with very thin wire.

## 2 more ideas...

- Make your table even more exquisite by using this same technique on a candle or vase.

- For a more elegant look, use pearl beads and wrap around a damask napkin.

# pumpkin decorating fun

Carved, painted, or donned with sequins, these **star-struck pumpkins** are stunning alone or in a grouping.

**To make the pumpkins you will need:**
Pumpkins of all sizes
Paint pen in desired color (often used for fabric painting, available at fabric, discount, and crafts stores)
Small paring knife
Votive candle
Star sequins
Straight pins with colored pearl ends
Small star cookie cutter

**here's how** **To make a paint-pen pumpkin,** draw stars in desired colors all over the pumpkin.

**To make a candleholder pumpkin,** cut a round hole (large enough to hold a votive candle) with a paring knife in the top of the pumpkin and scoop out. Decorate around the hole with paint pen as desired. Place a votive candle into the hole.

**To make a sequined pumpkin,** attach star sequins using straight pins with pearl ends.

**To make a cookie-cutter pumpkin,** press the star cookie cutter into the surface of the pumpkin and remove the "skin" of the star shape using a small paring knife.

## 2 more ideas...

- Wind the ends of a metallic pipe cleaner around a pencil, slip off, and attach a pipe cleaner to the stem of a miniature pumpkin.

- Attach a purchased artificial fall leaf at the stem of the pumpkin and display in a small pile of leaves.

# polished *terra-cotta* pot

Jazz up a terra-cotta pot with the help of a
*simple leaf pattern* and a touch
of shoe polish.

### To make the pot you will need:

Tracing paper
Clean terra-cotta pot with or without metal band
Contact paper (available at discount, hardware, and home center stores)
Masking tape
Spoon for burnishing
Paste shoe polish in colors cordovan and black
Clean, soft cloth
Clear varathane spray (available at craft and discount stores)
Small paintbrush

**1** **Trace leaf patterns,** *above,* and cut out. From Contact paper, cut out as many leaves as necessary to go around the container, using half small leaves and half large leaves.

**2** **Add vertical strips** of masking tape around the rim of the container.

**3** **Remove the backing from the smaller leaves** and evenly arrange the leaves around the pot and burnish (rub down) all edges using a spoon.

**5** **Remove the backing from the larger leaves** and arrange them around the pot between two of the smaller leaves, overlapping the edges of the small leaves. Burnish the edges. Apply a coat of black polish over the pot, avoiding the striped rim. Allow to dry.

**6** **Remove all of the Contact paper** and masking tape.

**4** **With the cloth,** apply a coat of cordovan color polish over the entire pot. Do not remove the Contact paper leaves. Allow the shoe polish to dry.

**7** **Add details** to the leaves using a paintbrush and cordovan color shoe polish. Spray the pot with varathane spray.

## 1 more idea...

• Use vinyl lettering instead of Contact paper designs to spell out messages or names on your terra-cotta pot.

## also try this...

• Turn your terra-cotta pot into a one-of-a-kind serving piece by placing a plastic liner in it before you fill it with food.

# good ideas *autumn candles*

Celebrate autumn by burning candles tucked into popcorn kernels, or surrounded by candy or mixed nuts. Have an extra bowl of goodies ready so little hands aren't tempted to touch.

# *glistening* fall trims

Relish the beauty of our natural
surroundings by preserving these
breathtaking wonders
in a coat of wax.

These wax-dipped remembrances of autumn add a gorgeous touch to fall arrangements or best-friend gifts.

**To make the trims you will need:**

Natural findings such as leaves, corn, and sunflowers
Raffia
Candle wax or parafin
Empty coffee can
Old pan
Hot plate or stove
Dowel
Newspapers
Brown paper sacks

**1** **Collect favorite fall items.** Tie a piece of raffia to the found nature items. *Note:* We tied two items, one on each end, to the raffia for ease in hanging.

**2** **Break up wax** and place in a clean coffee can. Put the coffee can in a pan of water to melt the wax, being careful not to overheat. Turn off the heat. Dip the items in wax.

**3** **Hang the items over a dowel** to dry, covering the surface below with newspapers to catch any drips. To display, hang wax-dipped items on a tree branch painted white or tie to a brown paper sack or wrapped package to make an interesting gift presentation.

## 1 more idea...
● Experiment with different nature items, including greens, pinecones, flowers, and shells.

## also try this...
● Use your wax-dipped naturals to decorate a Christmas tree, wreath, or mix in with fresh flowers and greens.

*sparkling*
beaded fruit

Purchased artificial miniature fruits get a glittery coat when covered with tiny glass beads.

**To make the fruit you will need:**
Small artificial fruit
Tacky glue
Toothpick
6mm colored beads to match color of fruit

**1** **Spread glue** onto the fruit using a toothpick.

**2** **Add beads,** one at a time, with holes facing out. Allow the glue to dry. Mix the colors of beads to resemble the natural color gradations of the fruit.

## 1 more idea...
● Use this same technique to add sparkle to other shapes, such as plastic stars or balls.

## also try this...
● Attach a hanging loop to make a glistening tree ornament or gift trim.

# cornucopia name cards

A purchased crocheted doily and a tiny bouquet of flowers fill a miniature cornucopia, inviting guests to gather and give thanks.

## To make the cornucopias you will need:

Miniature cornucopias
Purchased crocheted doilies
Small dried flowers
Scraps of solid color paper
Decorative-edged scissors

**here's how** **To make this project** simply tuck a small crocheted doily into the cornucopia. Poke the stems of the dried flowers into the doily, filling the cornucopia as desired. To personalize each place setting, use decorative-edged scissors to cut small rectangles from paper scraps. Write a guest's name on each scrap. Tuck the nameplates into the mini arrangements.

## 2 more ideas...

• Make a coordinating centerpiece by filling a large cornucopia with a mixture of large and small dried flowers.

• If you can't find miniature cornucopias, you can also use small grapevine wreaths, bottles, napkin rings—even metallic cupcake liners or pilgrim hats will hold the bouquets.

# nature's own seed ornaments

A simple cookie-cutter shape

## becomes the pattern

for these seed-covered

### trims of texture.

**here's how** **To make this project** trace around the cookie cutters onto cardboard and cut out the shapes. Glue the seeds onto the cardboard as desired, overlapping as necessary. To make the hanging loop, cut a 16-inch length of cord and fold it in half. Make a knot near the fold to make a loop for hanging. Glue the loose ends of the cord around the ornament, starting at the top and ending at the bottom. Trim off the ends of the cord so they meet each other.

## 1 more idea...
• Treat the birds by using toasted bread and peanut butter instead of cardboard and glue.

## also try this...
• Use a tweezers to make handling the smaller seeds easier.

# jack-o'-lantern *trim*

# The art of etching turns an ordinary clear glass ball into a jolly jack-o'-lantern.

**1** **Clean glass with hot water** and white vinegar. *Important:* Avoid finger prints on areas to be etched. Using tracing paper, trace the pattern, *below*.

**To make the ornament you will need:**

Clear glass round ornament
White vinegar
Tracing paper
Carbon paper
Contact® paper (available at discount, hardware, and home center stores)
X-Acto knife (available at art and crafts stores)
Spoon for burnishing
Rubber gloves
Etching cream (available at crafts stores)
Paintbrush with natural bristles or a sponge brush
Leaf
Natural raffia

**Placing carbon paper between the tracing and Contact paper,** trace the pattern onto the Contact paper. Cut out shapes using an X-Acto knife and remove the pieces. Stick the Contact paper pattern on the ornament, clipping the edges as necessary so the paper lays flat. Burnish (rub down) the paper using a spoon. **2**

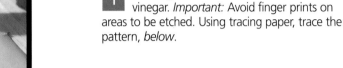

**3** **Put on rubber gloves** and paint on the etching cream following the instructions on the jar of etching cream.

**4** **Rinse off the etching cream** with water and remove the Contact paper. Tie a leaf and a few strips of raffia to the top of the ornament.

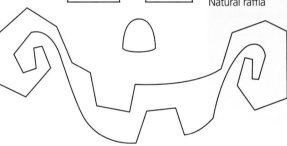

## 1 more idea...
● Use this same technique on a rose bowl and fill with candy for a special Halloween gift.

## also try this...
● For additional Halloween motifs, try etching bats, cats, and ghosts on your glass ornaments.

Complete with its bark and natural imperfections, a small log makes a rustic candle holder with a row of holes simply drilled into the top. Try various kinds of wood such as birch, oak, or pine.

# good ideas *woodsy candle holders*

# gifts for the birds

Get their little **hearts fluttering** with these clever and good-for-them **bird treats.**

**To make these bird treats you will need:**
Bagels
Peanut butter
 or thick honey
Birdseed
Cording
Ears of corn
Medium-weight wire
Red ribbon
Cereal
Dental floss
Sewing needle
Apples

**here's how** **To make bagel treats,** simply cut the bagels in half. Spread the cut side with either peanut butter or thick honey. Sprinkle with birdseed. To make a hanger, thread a short length of cording through the center hole in the bagel and knot the ends.

**To make corn treats**, wrap wire around the top of the cob, leaving a loop for hanging. Tie a red ribbon bow to the wire.

**To make cereal garlands,** cut a long length of dental floss and thread it into a needle. String dry cereal on the floss. Group the garlands together when hanging on the tree.

**To make apple treats,** cut a short length of wire and fold it in half. Wrap the loose ends of the wire around the apple stem, leaving a loop for hanging. *Note:* If using wire to hang the treats, be sure to secure the wire to the tree so it cannot be removed by the birds.

## 1 more idea...
● Use yarn to hang the treats—the birds will be able to recycle it in their nests in the spring.

## also try this...
● Birds will also love seed-covered stale bread hanging on a tree.

# more ideas *for* fall

- With a pail in hand, take a nature walk to collect fallen leaves, pinecones, acorns, and other autumn findings.

- After Halloween, watch for sales on holiday craft supplies and stock up for next year's ghoulish celebrations.

- Replace summer tapers and votives with candles in the colors of autumn.

- When school begins, tie an autumn plaid bow (see *page 93*) adorned with pencils and rulers to hang from your front door.

- Scatter a few colorful fall leaves on tabletops, in hutches, and around a gathering of gourds or pumpkins.

- Purchase a cassette tape of nature sounds set to music to play while crafting.

- Welcome guests with a collection of gourds and pumpkins arranged near the front steps or along the front walkway.

- Fill candy jars with mixed nuts and candy corn.

- Wire autumn findings to plant pokes to add a seasonal touch to plants and indoor floral arrangements.

- Pick up sale-priced paper goods, such as Halloween and Thanksgiving napkins and cups.

- Get out the warm throws to cuddle up with during the cool nights.

- Start collecting wood for cold-weather fires in the fireplace.

*If you can dream it,*

*you can do it.*

—— WALT DISNEY

# winter

The excitement of the season is enhanced by making handmade gifts to give and decorations to showcase your holiday home. Fill your days with the sparkle and merriment of the days of winter.

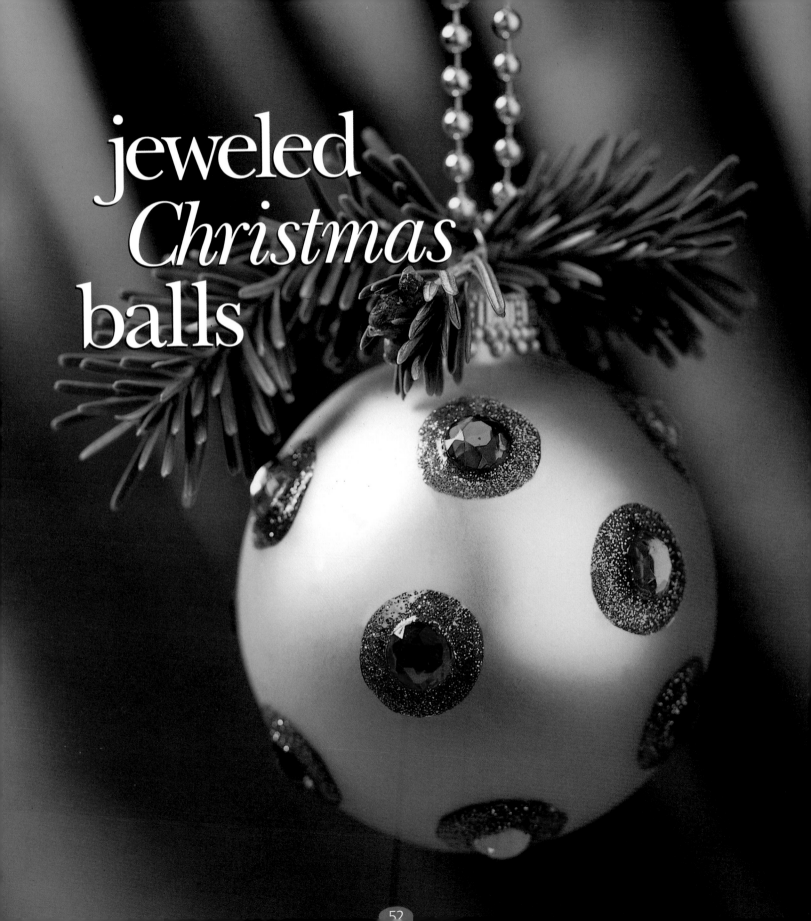

jeweled *Christmas* balls

Dressed up in jewels for the holidays, these quick-to-make ornaments will be the star attraction on your Christmas tree this season.

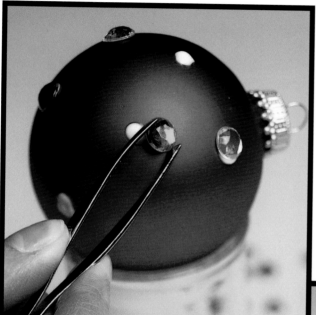

**To make the ornaments you will need:**
Solid-colored round Christmas ornament
Juice glass
Tweezers
Round jewels (available in crafts and discount stores)
Tacky glue
Gold glitter paint pen (available in crafts, discount, and fabric stores)

**1** **Place a Christmas ornament** on a juice glass to keep it from rolling. Using tweezers, arrange the jewels on the top half of the ball, securing the jewels with tacky glue. Let the glue dry.

**2** **To outline the jewels,** paint around each jewel using glitter paint pen, carefully circling jewel shape. (*Note:* Glitter paint will appear white until dry.) Let the paint dry. Repeat for the opposite side of the ornament.

## 1 more idea...
● Add a festive flare to a wall mirror by framing it in glitter-set jewels.

## also try this...
● Make color-coordinated candlesticks for any special occasion using this same quick-to-do embellishing technique.

## make it in minutes

# sparkling beaded candleholder

Reflect upon the season and create
our colorful beaded candleholder.

**To make the candleholders you will need:**

Beading wire (available in crafts and discount stores)
Glass or plastic beads as desired
Glass votive candleholder
Hot-glue gun and hot-glue sticks

## 1 more idea...

● To cover a larger candleholder with beaded wire, simply make several lengths and glue in the same manner as for the small votive candleholder.

## also try this...

● Try this same idea using miscellaneous jewelry findings, shells, and shank buttons.

**here's how** **To make this project** cut a piece of wire approximately 36 inches long. Place one bead on the end of the wire threading the wire through the bead a second time to secure. String beads on wire as desired, securing last bead as done for the first. Wrap beaded wire around candleholder to determine the placement. If you desire more length, simply cut and bead an extra length of wire. Secure one end of beaded wire with glue at the top edge of the candleholder. Wrap the beaded wire around the candleholder, securing with glue about every inch.

# cookie cutter candles

Choose your favorite holiday motif from the
cookie cutter drawer to make these holiday candles.

**To make the candles you will need:**
Sheets of beeswax
  (available at
  crafts stores)
Cutting board
Cookie cutters
Candlewick
  (available at
  crafts stores)
Hair dryer

## 1 more idea...
● Cut out a single shape
  from the beeswax,
  hole-punch the top,
  and you have a fun
  holiday ornament.

## also try this...
● Keep watch for unusual
  cookie cutter shapes.
  A heart, clover, spade,
  and diamond would
  make great candles for
  your next card club
  get-together.

here's how   **To make this project** lay sheets of beeswax individually on a
cutting board. Using a cookie cutter, cut six shapes (or more if a
thicker candle is desired) from beeswax. For nonsymmetrical shapes, turn the wax
over if it has a "right" side, to cut half of the shapes.
  Sandwich the wick in the center of the wax layers, leaving ½ inch at the top of
the candle. Press the wax shapes together. (*Note:* If they don't stick together well
enough, heat slightly with a hair dryer.) To burn the candles, secure them on another
small piece of beeswax or on a nonflammable surface. *Note:* Do not leave the candles
burning unattended.

# good ideas *holiday mantels*

Simple collections make for stunning mantel
decorations. We've grouped glass finials, small snow-kissed
trees, and colorful bottles with pinecone stoppers atop our fireplace
mantels. You can rest your favorite collections on holiday greens and
garlands, or nothing at all for a more contemporary look.

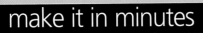
# ribbon poinsettia rings

Satin ribbon and beads combine to create

a most pleasing poinsettia napkin holder.

## To make a napkin holder you will need:

17½-inch piece of ⅝-inch-wide red wire-edged satin ribbon

17½-inch piece of ⅝-inch-wide forest green wire-edged taffeta ribbon

Straight pins

Red and gold sewing threads

Sewing needle

Mill Hill old gold (05557) glass beads

Metallic gold spray paint (available at crafts and discount stores)

Wood napkin ring

Hot-glue gun and hot-glue sticks

**here's how** **To make this project**

cut five 3½-inch lengths of red and of green ribbon for each napkin ring. Fold each length to make a petal as shown, *below left*. Stack five red petals so the ends overlap in the center and the folded points spread in a circle to form a poinsettia. Pin the ends together. Stitch through the center several times with red thread, securing ribbon ends. Trim off loose ends of ribbon. Remove the pin.

Place five green leaf petals under the red petals, spacing so that each leaf is between the red petals. Stitch through the center again, securing the red and green petals. Stitch gold pebble beads to the flower center with gold thread, covering the ribbon ends. Adjust the petals to make the flower dimensional. Spray the wood napkin ring with gold paint and let dry. Glue the poinsettia onto the napkin ring.

## 1 more idea...

● Make extra ribbon poinsettias to use as package trims, lapel pins, and Christmas tree ornaments.

## also try this...

● You can make other colors of poinsettias by replacing the red ribbon with white, burgundy, or variegated pink ribbon.

# holiday kitchen trims

Make a snowy evening seem warm and cozy

by creating this winter centerpiece.

Grater, sieve, or other kitchen tool
Artificial or real holly or other winter greenery
Hot-glue gun and hot-glue sticks
Candle (optional)

**here's how** **To make this project**
wash the kitchen tool well and let it dry. Arrange the greenery as desired and glue only the greenery together. Glue the arranged piece to the kitchen tool. Place a candle inside if desired.

## 1 more idea...
● For a Christmas decoration for the kitchen door, wire utensils to a purchased wreath or swag, adding torn fabric bows for color.

## also try this...
● Check the silver cabinet for decorative flatware and napkin rings as they can be wired into holiday centerpieces as well.

# marbleized
## centerpiece

# Metallic paints swirled inside crystal clear ornaments create a striking holiday centerpiece.

**To make the centerpiece you will need:**
Clear glass Christmas ornament with removable top
Liquid acrylic paint in desired colors (available at crafts and discount stores)

**1** **Remove the cap** from the ornament. Pour a small amount (about one teaspoon) of paint into the ornament. Using the same amount, add the second color of paint.

**2** **Turn the ornament around and around,** swirling the paint to make a marbleized affect. Leave the cap off of the ornament until the paint has dried. Replace the cap. Place the ornaments in a clear bowl with a purchased beaded garland.

## 1 more idea...
● To make a snowman ornament, paint the entire inside using white paint and then add a snowman's face to the outside using dots of black paint pen.

## also try this...
● Add a simple ribbon bow to the ornament cap before hanging on the tree or on a garland of holiday greenery.

good ideas *copycat package trims*

You can create package trims to use on any favorite gift wrap. Study the motif on the paper. We have chosen a fruit gift wrap, a holly wrap, and an angel with halo wrap. Using the motif as inspiration, glue a similar motif to the wrapped gift. We used purchased plastic fruit for the fruit motif, tiny silk holly for the holly wrap, and a halo we made by wrapping gold garland around a wire for the angel wrap. You can criss-cross a ribbon under the added motif or glue the motifs directly on the paper.

# candy-filled gifts

### Simple dime store cookie cutters make great gifts filled with favorite goodies.

**To make a candy treat you will need:**
Pencil
Open-style cookie cutter in desired shape
Lightweight cardboard
Scissors
Clear tape
Nuts or small candies in holiday colors
Corsage bag (available at floral shops)
8 inches of desired ribbon

**here's how** **To make this project**
draw around the cookie cutter onto the lightweight cardboard. Cut out the shape. Tape the cardboard to the back of the cookie cutter. Fill the cookie cutter with nuts or candies as desired. Leaving treat laying flat, slide the corsage bag around the cookie cutter and tie a ribbon bow around the open end of the bag.

## 2 more ideas...

● For a toddler's birthday, choose a cookie cutter in the shape of the child's age and fill with tiny treats.

● To personalize guest's place settings, use alphabet-shaped cookie cutters to spell out names, wrapping each letter separately in plastic wrap.

# scalloped
## paper
## gift tags

To: Holly
From: Pam

To: Tim
From: Amy

To: Li
From: Nick

To: Scott
From: SANTA

Snippets of paper trimmed with
**paper-punched lace edges** make
keepsake gift tags.

**To make the tags you will need:**
Scraps of paper in holiday colors and ivory or white
Straight and decorative-edged scissors (available in crafts and fabric stores)
Small round paper punch
Paper punches with desired shapes (available in crafts and discount stores)
Crafts glue

**1** **Using straight or decorative-edged** scissors, cut a desired shape from the ivory or white paper. *Note:* This is the piece of paper you will write on.

**2** **Using the gift tags,** *opposite,* for inspiration, cut additional shapes from colored papers. To hold paper layers together, punch two holes through layers and weave a paper strip through the holes to secure.

**3** **To make a lacy edge,** first cut the edge of the paper with a scalloped-edged scissors. Then, use a small paper punch to create holes within the scallops (see *above*).

**4** **To decorate the tags,** glue the decorative-shaped paper punches and the tiny pieces that have been punched away onto the cut shapes.

## 1 more idea...
● Make your own note cards, greeting cards, photo mats, and more using this fun technique.

## also try this...
● If you prefer to write on dark-colored papers, try writing with a pen that has silver, gold, or white ink.

# frosted
## ornament
## trims

# A touch of winter white
## is easy to mimmick when you etch
### simple glass ornaments.

**1** **Clean glass** with hot water and white vinegar. (*Important:* Avoid finger prints on areas to be etched.) Use paint pen to draw snowflake designs and/or masking tape to outline stripes. Press down star stickers to make star motifs. Be sure all tape or stickers are rubbed down. Allow the paint to dry. Refer to the etched ornaments, *opposite*, for ideas.

**2** **Put on gloves** and etch the glass following the instructions on the jar of etching cream.

**3** **Wash off the etching cream** and gently peel off the paint and/or stickers and tape. Thread the key chain through the ornament hanger and snap closed. Tuck a small sprig of greenery into the ornament top.

**To make an ornament you will need:**
Clear glass round Christmas ornament
White vinegar
¼-inch-wide masking tape
Paint pen (available in crafts, discount, and fabric stores)
Star stickers
Rubber gloves
Etching cream (available in art, crafts, and discount stores)
Paintbrush
Key chain
Sprig of greenery

## 1 more idea...
● You can also do this fun etching process on mirrors.

## also try this...
● To etch names or words, use vinyl press-on letters.

# mitten doorknob welcome

**To make the trim you will need:**

Scissors
Purchased mitten
Tissue paper
Greenery
Cinnamon sticks
Medium-weight wire
Wire cutters
Fabric bow

A simple mitten filled with goodies welcomes friends and family.

**here's how** **To make this project** stuff the mitten with tissue paper to give it shape, then fill it with greens and cinnamon sticks. If desired, add a wire hanger to the opposite sides of the mitten top, tying a fabric bow to one side of the hanger.

## 1 more idea...

● To wrap a tiny present or gift certificate, place it in this country-style mitten and attach a homespun bow.

## also try this...

● Make several of these mitten trims and use as decorations on your Christmas tree.

# gingerbread-friends garland

These gingerbread friends hold hands just to create a holiday garland for your mantel.

**To make the garland you will need:**
Gingerbread men cookies (decorated and with holes in hands)
⅛-inch-wide red ribbon
Scissors

**here's how** **To make this project**

make several gingerbread men cookies (see recipe on *page 216*) in the size desired. Before baking, use a straw to make a small hole in each hand. After the cookies have been baked and cooled, decorate as desired using icing. Connect the cookies together by threading thin ribbon through the holes in their hands. Knot the ribbon and trim the ends.

## 1 more idea...
● For a more lasting version, use oven-bake clay to make the gingerbread men.

## also try this...
● Other cookie cutter shapes would make cute garlands too—try reindeer, snowmen, or Santa boots!

Glass candleholders, vases, even ice cream dishes make clever holders for your favorite holiday ornaments. Embellish your arrangement with some sparkling garland

# good ideas *ornaments on display*

or colorful curly ribbon, and you're ready to spread holiday cheer in every room of the house.

# peppermint wreaths

**To make a wreath you will need:**

Tracing paper
Medium-weight cardboard
Scissors
¼-inch-wide red metallic ribbon
Hot-glue gun and hot-glue sticks
Small candy canes or peppermints

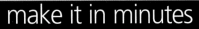

## 1 more idea...

- For an outdoor version of this wreath, use wrapped candies and secure them in place with clear thread instead of glue.

## also try this...

- For projects like this, pick up seasonal candies when they go on sale and keep them in a cool place until ready to use.

here's how **To make this project** trace desired size circle wreath pattern, *opposite*. Transfer to cardboard and cut out. Glue the end of the ribbon to the cardboard circle and wrap ribbon around the cardboard until it is entirely covered. Cut the ribbon and secure it to the cardboard with glue. Arrange candy on the circle and glue in place. Add a bow if desired.

# peppermint wreaths

fold

Candy canes and peppermints
line up to form festive
holiday trims.

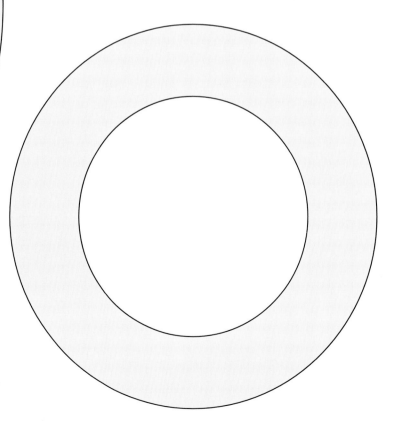

# good ideas *stocking surprise holders*

Purchased holiday-trimmed socks are a gift and the wrapping all in one. Just tuck special surprises inside and hide in the evergreen branches for little ones to discover on Christmas morning.

# good ideas *canning jar luminaries*

Fill canning jars with common, yet colorful non-flammable items. We've used buttons, candy, marbles, and aquarium rocks. Place a candle in a votive cup and nestle it in the middle of the jar for a glowing effect.

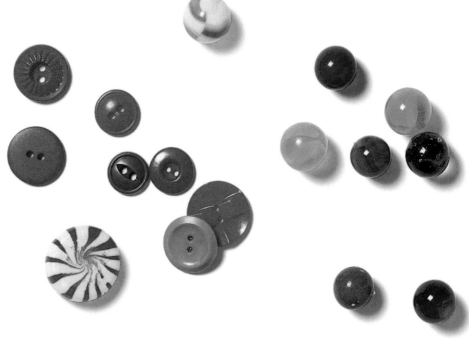

# from the country lampshade

Favorite winter motifs cut from felt

are all it takes to make your lamp

a shade better.

**To make the lampshade you will need:**

4-inch-high lampshade (available at discount and home center stores)
Paper
Sharp scissors
Tracing paper
8×16-inch piece of ivory felt
5×10-inch piece of green felt
2×5-inch piece of yellow felt
Fusible webbing (available at crafts, discount, and fabric stores)
Iron
Tacky glue

here's how **To make this project** lay the lampshade on its side on top of the piece of paper. Begin tracing the top and bottom, rolling it as you trace. Cut out the pattern and wrap it around the lampshade to determine the length around the shade. Use the paper pattern you've made to cut one piece from ivory felt.

Trace the tree and star designs, *below,* and cut seven trees from the green felt and nine stars from the yellow felt. Lay the ivory felt piece flat and arrange trees and stars on the ivory felt. Following instructions with the fusible webbing, fuse the trees and stars to the ivory felt.

Wrap the ivory piece around the lampshade, with the design side out and aligning the top and bottom edges with the edges of the shade. Glue in place.

## 1 more idea...
● To add a cheerful touch to a child's lamp, trace his or her hand to make bright colored felt cut outs.

## also try this...
● Make several themed lampshades to celebrate each new season.

Create a stunning tabletop by combining some of your favorite holiday decorations. In a variety of lovely shallow dishes, we've grouped

# good ideas *shimmering centerpieces*

ornaments, candles, and metallic beaded garlands. For the finishing touch, wrap several tapers together using non-flammable ribbon or cording. Be careful not to let the candles burn to within one inch of the ribbon. Do not leave the candles burning unattended.

# tiny mirror tree trims

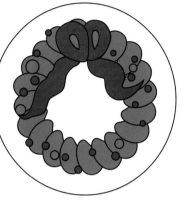

Reflect the holiday season
with a little painting magic.

**To make the trims you will need:**

Vinegar
Small beveled
  mirrors in desired
  shapes
Liquitex Glossies
  paint for glass
  (available in art
  and crafts stores)
Small round
  paintbrush
White felt
Cording

**here's how** **To make these projects** wash the mirrors and rinse them with vinegar. (*Important:* Do not get any fingerprints on the mirror fronts.) Let the mirrors dry thoroughly.

Using the samples and illustrated patterns, *pages 84–86,* for inspiration, paint desired designs on the mirrors. (If you want to practice, simply paint a mirror, then wash and rinse it again before the paint dries.) Let the paint dry.

Trace around the mirrors onto felt and cut out. Cut a 10-inch length of cording. Sandwich the ends of the cording between the mirror and the felt to make a hanging loop. Glue felt to back of the mirror and let it dry.

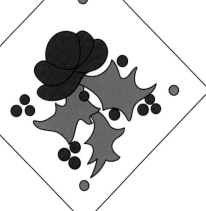

## 1 more idea...
● Set in a tiny easel, these mirrors make elegant place cards.

## also try this...
● Try this same painting technique on a larger mirror to create a beautiful perfume tray.

# tiny mirror tree trims
(continued)

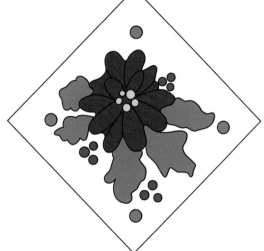

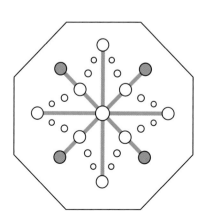

# Christmas-candy topiary

Sweets from the season combine to make a most unexpected holiday gift.

**here's how** **To make this project** mix a batch of Royal Frosting (see recipe on *page 216*). To 1½ cups of frosting, add more confectioner's sugar as necessary to make frosting very stiff. Remove paper wraps from candies, if necessary. Working from top, spread a liberal amount of frosting 2 inches down the sides of one cone. Using photo, *left*, for ideas, begin to arrange candies around cone. Repeat until the cone is covered with candies. When completed, set the cone on a piece of plastic wrap and allow it to dry thoroughly.

Cut off the top of second cone so that the bottom fits in mug. Wedge Styrofoam into mug, securing it with frosting if needed.

Cut off curved portion of candy cane. Push the cane gently into the bottom of the decorated cone at the center. Remove and push it into the center of the Styrofoam in the mug. Remove again and put crafts glue into the hole in the Styrofoam in the mug. Place cane in glue and let dry.

In a small bowl, mix ¼ cup of water and several drops of green food coloring. Add ½ cup coconut and stir to distribute color evenly. Spread on a piece of foil on a cookie sheet. Bake at 200° for 20–30 minutes, checking frequently, until coconut is dry. Remove from oven.

Put glue into the hole in the bottom of the cone and place atop candy cane. Prop up if necessary until set. Fill mug with colored coconut.

**To make the topiary you will need:**
- 1 recipe Royal Frosting (see page 216)
- Confectioner's sugar
- Assorted candies
- 2 small Styrofoam tree-shaped cones (available at crafts and discount stores)
- Plastic wrap
- Purchased Christmas coffee mug
- Large candy cane
- Crafts glue
- Small bowl
- Water
- Green food coloring
- Shredded coconut
- Tin foil
- Cookie sheet
- Oven

## 1 more idea...
- Use egg-shaped Styrofoam, Easter candies, and a colorful candy stick for a springtime version of this topiary.

## also try this...
- Try other small containers such as clay pots, votive candleholders, or sugar bowls to use as the base.

# pleated
## golden
*ornament*

# Shimmering fabric and a lonely clip earring come together to make a keepsake ornament.

**1** **Sew the short ends** of the lamé together, making a tube. Hand-sew running stitches along the top and bottom raw edges. Gather the bottom thread. From inside the tube, push the tassel hanger through the gathers. Stitch to secure. Turn lamé tube right side out.

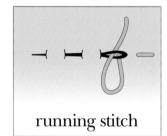

running stitch

**To make the ornament you will need:**
3½-inch-diameter Styrofoam ball
7x9-inch piece of pleated gold lamé (available at fabric stores)
Thread
Needle
18 inches of gold cording
18 inches of 1-inch-wide burgundy ribbon
Clip earring or lapel pin
2-inch-long metallic gold tassel

**2** **Put the Styrofoam ball inside** the tube. Gather the running stitches. Cut a 6-inch length of gold cording for the hanger. Tuck the ends of the cording into the gathers. Stitch to secure.

**3** **Tie the burgundy ribbon** into a bow over the running stitches. Tie the remaining 12 inches of cording into a bow beneath the ribbon bow. Pin or clip the jewelry piece to the center of the bows.

## 1 more idea...
● To create your own jewelry-like trims, glue packaged gems to a small cardboard shape and outline each with glitter paint pen.

## also try this...
● Without the hanging loop and tassel, these golden ornaments look elegant displayed in a crystal pedestal dish.

# *blossoming bow* door trims

Beckon guests inside with a surprise-laden holiday bow nestled in a few sprigs from an evergreen tree.

Turn the page for more bow ideas and step-by-step instructions.

# blossoming bow trims

(continued)

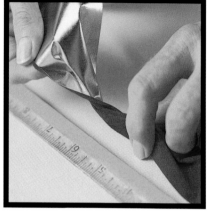

**2** Make a **6-inch loop,** bring it back to the center, and twist and pinch the ribbon again.

**To make the bow trims you will need:**

4 to 5 yards of 2½- to 3-inch-wide ribbon

12-inch ruler

Pipe cleaners

Wire or hot-glue gun and hot-glue sticks, if desired

**1** Starting with all of the ribbon yardage, measure 15 inches from one end and lay the ribbon by the ruler with that point at the 6-inch mark. Twist and pinch ribbon here.

**3** Make **another 6-inch loop** on the opposite side and bring it to the center, twisting and pinching again.

**4** Make **eight or ten loops,** alternating sides.

**5** Secure the bow loops by twisting a pipe cleaner around the center of the bow.

**6** Tie an extra length of ribbon around the center of the bow and trim the ribbon ends. Attach desired trims using wire or hot glue.

## 1 more idea...

● To make a warm-weather version of this door trim, use artificial flowers tucked into a few sprigs of artificial ivy.

## also try this...

● Use these festive bows as tree toppers or as special trims for railings, fences and gates—even the mailbox post.

# *bauble* dress up

# Tiny dots of paint is all it takes
## to make our plain ornament
## oh so fancy.

**To make an ornament you will need:**
Clear glass Christmas ornament
Glitter paint pen, if desired (available in crafts and discount stores)
1 yard of 2- to 3-inch-wide wire-edged or stiff ribbon
Thin wire
Hot-glue gun and hot-glue sticks
1 yard *each* of one or two contrasting narrower ribbons
Small glass or acrylic balls or other small desired trims
Small beads

**1** **To make this project** add dots or other designs to the glass ornament using glitter paint pen. Let the paint pen dry completely.

**2** **Make three to six large loops of ribbon** leaving long tails. Pinch the center of the ribbons and wrap with wire to secure. Glue the ribbon bow to the top of the ball.

**3** **Shape smaller ribbons** into loops, wire together, and glue to the base of the large ribbon loops. Glue small balls, or other desired trims, to the ribbons. Use glitter paint as glue and add small beads to the bows and ornaments, if desired.

## 1 more idea...
● For a more natural look, substitute materials such as raffia, pinecones, dried flowers, and shells for the narrow ribbons and the small glass and acrylic ornaments.

## also try this...
● To make an elegant centerpiece, nestle a few of these sparkling balls in a crystal bowl filled with sprigs of evergreen.

When you lovingly choose gifts for family and friends, make sure the wrap is just as special. Here we've wrapped our gifts in metallic papers and then trimmed them with doily placemats, circles, squares, and hearts. Though inexpensive to purchase, these lacy accents give our gifts an elegant finale.

good ideas *fancy doily wraps*

# simply sparkling prisms

**To make a
prism trim you
will need:**
Chandelier prism
(available at
home center
stores)
Wire ornament
hanger
12-inch piece
of ribbon

Catch the light

of the season

by hanging this

pretty prism.

**here's how** **To make this project**
attach an ornament
hanger to the top of the prism. Tie a
dainty bow at the top, letting the ribbon
ends trail down the sides of the prism.

## 1 more idea...
● Attach this gem of a
trim to a special
package at
Christmastime.

## also try this...
● Use this same technique
to create one-of-a-kind
trims using odds 'n'
ends of jewelry.

# jingle bell trim

Dress up
a jolly bell to
**ring in**
the holiday
season.

**To make this trim you will need:**

Lightweight wire
Wire cutters
Red berry cluster
Sprigs of evergreen
Large gold jingle-bell ornament (available at crafts and fabric stores)
1¼ yards of 2-inch-wide sheer ribbon

**here's how** **To make this project** wire the berry cluster and the evergreen sprigs together, then wire them to the hanging loop of the jingle-bell ornament. Thread the ribbon through the hanging loop. Knot and tie a bow in the ribbon about 7 inches from the ornament.

## 1 more idea...

- Using stocking holders, hang these festive trims from a mantle.

## also try this...

- Add a sprig of mistletoe and hang from the top of a doorway for a music-making holiday kissing ball.

# *keepsake* rose hearts

# Glorious roses tucked together into a heart shape create a most elegant Valentine.

fold

**To make a rose heart you will need:**

Typing or tracing paper
Floral oasis foam (available at crafts, discount, or florist stores)
Tacky glue, if desired
Water
Pie tin
About one dozen miniature or small roses in desired color
Sharp knife
Fresh lemon leaves (available at flower shops)
Pins

**1** **Trace pattern** onto typing or tracing paper. Place the pattern over the oasis and cut out the heart shape. (*Note:* If oasis is not big enough, oasis may be glued together.) Put water in the pie tin and soak the oasis in water for about ½ hour.

**2** **Cut off heads of roses** and place into the oasis filling in space as tightly as possible.

**After the entire oasis** **3** is filled with flower heads, turn the heart on its side and pin lemon leaves around the sides, overlapping as needed. Continue until the oasis is entirely covered.

**Place the floral heart** **4** on a glass or china plate or in a shallow bowl.

# 1 more idea...
● For an everlasting version of this rose heart, use freeze-dried or silk roses.

# also try this...
● To add a message to this romantic gift, write it on a ribbon using a paint pen and attach the small banner across the top.

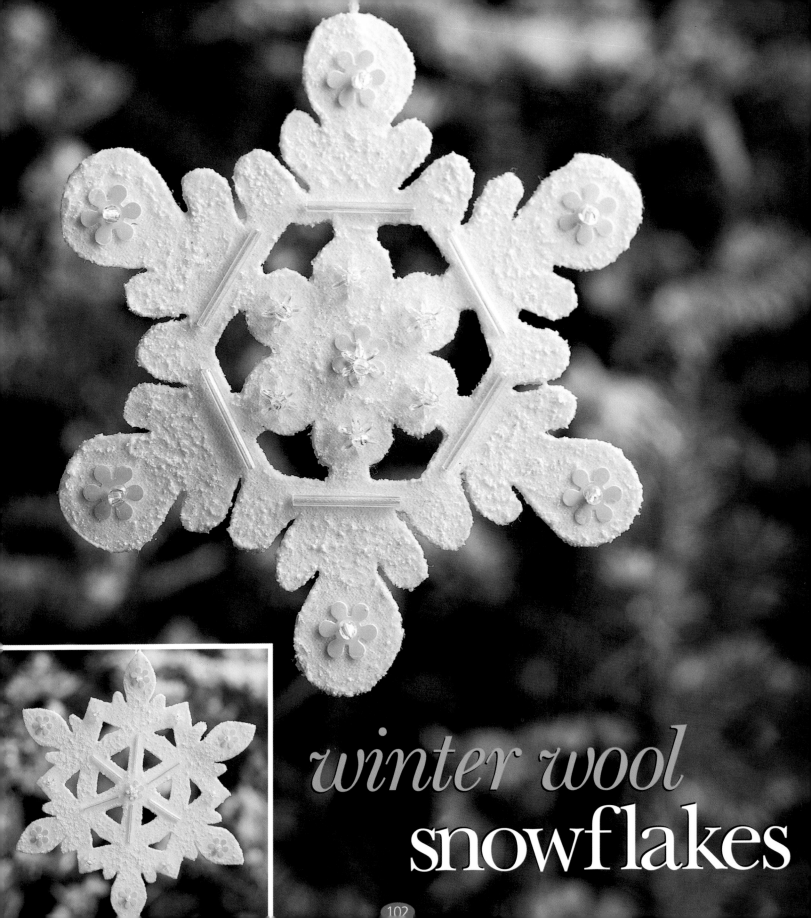

*winter wool*
snowflakes

Pure white woolen fabric, beads, and glitter
make these snowflakes sparkle.

**1** **Trace desired snowflake**
pattern, *pages 104–105*, onto
tracing paper. Transfer to fusible webbing.
Fuse to the wrong side of the wool fabric
following the manufacturer's directions.

**2** **Cut out**
the snowflake
shape from the
fused wool fabric.

**To make a
snowflake you
will need:**
Tracing paper
Heavy-weight fusible
  webbing
Iron
Medium-weight
  white wool
Scissors
White Duncan
  SnowWriters
  paint pen (available
  at crafts stores)
1-inch crystal bugle
  beads
⅜-inch clear-plastic
  star beads
Large crystal seed
  beads
½-inch sew-on
  white iris sequin
  snowflakes
12 inches ⅛-inch-wide
  ribbon
White thread
Beading needle
Paintbrush

**Cut out** the **4**
snowflake
shape a second
time, being careful
not to cut off the
hanging loop.

**3** **Remove the backing**
from the fusible
webbing. Place the ends of
the ribbon on the webbing at
the top of the snowflake,
overlapping the edge about
½ inch to make a hanging
loop. Fuse the snowflake
shape to another piece of
wool fabric so both the front
and the back of the snowflake
is wool.

**5** **Seal the raw edges**
of the snowflake using
paint pen. Let the paint dry.
Stitch beads to the snowflake
as shown on the patterns,
*pages 104–105.* Use a
paintbrush to add paint to
the surface of the snowflake.

# 1 more idea...
● Cut snowflakes from
  paper instead of fabric
  and attach them to a
  plain colored notecard
  to make a special
  holiday greeting card.

# also try this...
● To enjoy all winter long,
  use these glistening
  snowflakes to trim
  table linens.

# winter wool snowflakes

(continued)

*valentine* frame

# Preserve a love token and keep it always
## by etching your own winter frosted frame.

**1** **Clean the glass portion of frame** with hot water and white vinegar. *Important:* Do not get any fingerprints on areas to be etched.

**2** **From a piece of paper,** cut the desired mat size and divide the sides into equal sections. Place this paper under the glass and use ¼-inch-wide masking tape to tape diagonal lines in each section.

**3** **Draw heart patterns** onto the Contact paper and cut out using a crafts knife or use heart stickers. Peel the backing from the Contact paper or stickers and center the hearts as desired in taped-off areas on the glass. Some of the edges might need to be clipped to enable the Contact paper to lay flat. Burnish (rub down) all of the edges of the Contact paper with a spoon, avoiding putting fingerprints on the glass.

**4** **Add dots around** the hearts in the outside corners with the paint pen. Allow to thoroughly dry before etching.

**5** **Wearing rubber gloves,** paint etching cream over tape and Contact paper according to manufacturer's instructions. Leave on for about 5 minutes.

**6** **Rinse the glass thoroughly** and remove the tape, paint, and Contact paper. Center the card or message on colored paper or sheet of foam. Assemble the frame.

## To make the frame you will need:

Clear-glass frame with a clip-on back
White vinegar
Paper
Ruler
¼-inch-wide masking tape
Contact paper
Crafts knife
Heart stickers, if desired
Spoon for burnishing
Paint pen (usually used for fabric, available in crafts, discount, and fabric stores)
Rubber gloves
Etching cream
Paintbrush
Colored paper or foam sheet (available at crafts and discount stores)

## 1 more idea...

● Using vinyl stick-on letters, etch a name or sentimental message onto the frame.

## also try this...

● Because you can customize your frame, this technique works great to capture a theme of a photograph or treasured greeting card.

# sweetheart candy wreath

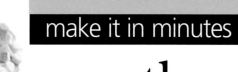

The conversation is sure to be sweet after you create this clever candy wreath.

**here's how** **To make this project** wrap the wreath with ribbon and secure with glue. Arrange hearts onto the ribbon-covered wreath and glue the candies atop the ribbon, overlapping as desired.

## 1 more idea...

• For Halloween, choose an autumn-inspired ribbon and top with candy corn.

## also try this...

• Turn this tiny wreath into a sweet candle ring by laying it flat to encircle a pillar candle.

# heartthrob pins

A **most unusual** and clever technique creates
**glittering hearts** to wear and cherish.

**1** **Add enough Mod Podge** to the couscous pasta to hold it together well; stir and mix thoroughly. *Note:* Don't allow the mixture to sit long as it tends to harden quickly.

**Spoon pasta mixture onto wooden** heart. **2**
Shape and mold the pasta quickly with fingers, pressing it firmly together and onto the heart shape. Allow to dry.

**3** **Paint pasta with acrylic paint,** sprinkling glitter onto the wet paint. Let the paint dry. Trim the outside edge with braid using tacky glue to secure. Glue a satin ribbon rose to the front as desired. Secure a pin back on the back side of the heart shape using tacky glue.

**To make a pin you will need:**
Bowl
Spoon
Mod Podge decoupage medium
Couscous pasta
Small wood heart shape (available at crafts and discount stores)
Acrylic paint in desired color
Glitter
Braid trim
Tacky glue
Satin rose
Pin back

## 1 more idea...
● Spruce up a tired old frame by embellishing it with painted couscous.

## also try this...
● Pasta pins can be made using any wood shape—try an egg shape for Easter or a wreath shape for Christmas.

Mismatched goblets come together beautifully to create a stunning centerpiece. To make this project, fill the goblets with water. Float the candles in the water and add a shake of confetti in each goblet. Arrange the goblets on a tray, mantel, or center of a table. Light the candles for a glorious centerpiece.

good ideas *goblet centerpiece*

winter *luminaries*

Lackluster tin cans come alive with a unique piercing technique and candlelight.

Any size tin can
Water
Hammer
Large nail
Medium-gauge wire
Large screw eye
Vise
Drill
2×2-inch scrap of wood
Needle-nose pliers
Sand
Votive candles
Red ribbon
Greenery

**1** **Fill the tin can with water** and freeze. Use hammer and nail to make holes around rim, about ½ inch from top of can.

**4** **From the outside of the tin can,** slip the uncurled wire ends through one hole, then through a hole on the opposite side. Curl the remaining wire ends into spirals.

**5** **Pull the handle up** through the top of the can. (Note: Be careful of sharp edges on the can and wire.) On each 4-inch length of wire, make a bend about ½ inch in from the end (to create a hook for third curled wire) to slip into each handle hole. Curl the opposite ends. Slip hook end of each curled wire into a handle hole.

**2** **Cut the wire into one** 36-inch length and two 4-inch lengths. For the handle, fold the 36-inch length in half. Thread the wire through the screw eye. Clamp at least 2 inches of the wire (the cut ends) in a vise.

**3** **Insert the screw eye** into the drill chuck and tighten. Begin twisting the wire handle by running the drill. After a few twists are in the wire, slip the wood scrap between the end of the loop and the twists. Continue twisting the wire by running the drill until the length is evenly twisted. Remove the wire from the vise and remove the wood scrap. Cut the loop, then use pliers to curl the wire ends at one end into spirals. Note: Do not curl the opposite ends yet.

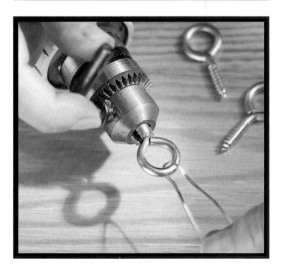

**6** **Fill the can** with sand and add candles. Using ribbon, tie a bow around can. Tuck a small piece of greenery between can and the bow.

## 1 more idea...
● Use water and floating candles instead of sand and votives for unique indoor luminaries.

## also try this...
● You can also drill the holes in the can—except do not use the frozen water method and always wear eye protection when using electric tools.

# good ideas *garlands of fun*

As much fun to string as they are to decorate with, these unexpected garlands are made up of caramel corn, colored popcorn, corks and beads, bright-colored jelly beans, and miniature artificial fruits. Use your imagination when stringing your next garland, you might want to try small shells or jingle bells!

# heart of my heart pillow

Easy-to-make yet lacy and proper, this pillow will be dear to your heart.

**To make the pillow you will need:**

¼ yard of cardinal red felt

8-inch white Battenburg lace heart (available at crafts and discount stores)

Straight pins

2 feet of ¼-inch-wide pale pink pearl string

Pale pink sewing thread

1½-inch-long burgundy tassel

⅛-inch-wide Kreinik Metallics ribbon in color 193 pale mauve

Fiberfill

#20 chenille needle

**here's how** **To make this project** cut two pieces of felt 8½x9 inches. Center the Battenburg heart on one of the felt pieces and pin. Pin the pearl string around the inside edge of the heart. Start the end in the top center of the heart, with the end curled into a "C" on one side and ending with a reverse "C" on the other side.

With coordinating thread, stitch the bead string in place going through the Battenburg and felt. Fold the tassel loop behind the tassel and stitch it to the tassel with a couple of stitches. Place the tassel centered between the two pearl string curves. Stitch it to the Battenburg and felt behind the top head of the tassel. Pin the heart top to the second piece of felt. Stitch together with a running stitch ⅓ inch from the edge with pale mauve metallic ⅛-inch-wide ribbon. Stop stitching 4 inches from the beginning. Stuff the pillow with fiberfill. Continue stitching to the starting point.

**running stitch**

## 1 more idea...
- Embroider a name or sweet message on the pillow front for a personalized keepsake.

## also try this...
- For an elegant Victorian look, replace the felt with dainty vintage handkerchiefs or cloth napkins.

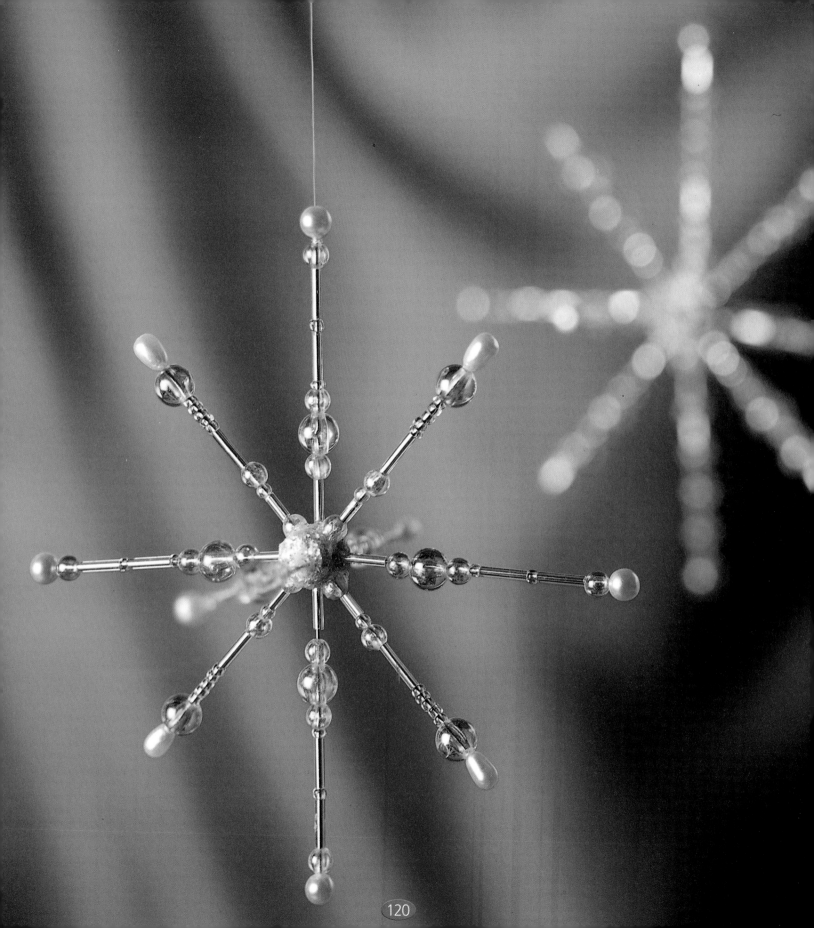

# beaded snowflakes

The light will dance
on these wintertime snowflakes,
made from a variety of
crystal-like beads.

**To make the snowflakes you will need:**
Corsage pins with pearl ends (available in fabric and craft stores)
Crystal-like beads in desired shapes and sizes
Small cork
Iridescent white glitter paint pen (usually used for fabric, available in craft and discount stores)
Monofilament thread

**here's how** **To make this project** place beads on one corsage pin in desired order, leaving the last ¼ inch without beads. Make three more beaded pins using the same arrangement. Make another set of four beaded pins, using a different arrangement. Make an additional set of two beaded pins. (You should have a total of ten beaded pins.)

Cut the cork, if necessary, so it is about ¼ inch long. With the round side of the cork laying on the work surface, poke one beaded pin into the cork (close to work surface) like a spoke of a wheel. Place a matching beaded pin opposite the first. Place the remaining two opposite each other, between the first set.

Using the remaining set of four, poke each into the cork, slightly closer to the top of the cork and alternating with the first set of four. Place the remaining two beaded pins into each round end of the cork.

Cover the cork using glitter paint pen. Allow to dry. Apply a second coat, if necessary, and let dry.

To hang, cut a desired length of monofilament and tie to one spoke of the snowflake.

## 1 more idea...
● If the kids want to make these snowflakes, use pipe cleaners instead of pins and Styrofoam balls instead of corks.

## also try this...
● These sparkling snowflakes also stand on their own for a lovely wintertime centerpiece.

# snow-covered candle toppers

Create your own version of sparkling
snow and let it fall wherever
you choose.

**To make the
toppers you
will need:**
Epsom salt
Bowl
White wine
Assorted clear glass
   candle holders,
   globes, or
   ornaments
Pie tin
Paintbrush
Candles, if desired

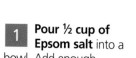

**1** **Pour ½ cup of
Epsom salt** into a
bowl. Add enough
wine to make a slush from
the salt.

**Hold the
glass piece** **2**
over a pie tin
when applying
the Epsom salt
mixture. Using the
paintbrush, pat
the slush onto the
outside of the
glass piece as
desired. *Note:* If
the slush slides off,
let the glassware
dry on one side
until the slush
begins to harden.
Then turn it and
apply the slush to
the remaining area.

**3** **Let the
glassware
dry** overnight
until the slush
hardens. To
remove the slush,
run warm water
over the outside
of the glass piece.

## 1 more idea...
● "Frost" your windows
with Epsom salt for a
sparkling wintry effect.

## also try this...
● Try this technique on
colored glassware and
surround with miniature
Christmas lights for a
colorful glow.

*silvery*
tree candle
covers

# Twinkling light shines through tiny holes
## of our magical tree-shaped covers.

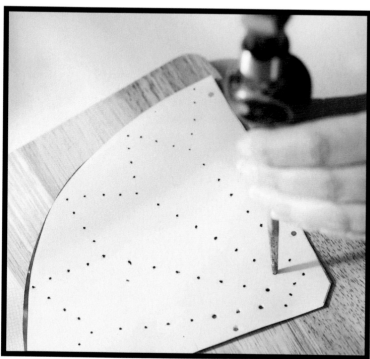

**1** **Before beginning,** trace and cut a paper pattern using the pattern on *page 126*, and make sure it fits over the top edge of the glass votive holder. Make any necessary size adjustments.

**2** **Trace around the paper** pattern on a piece of tooling foil. Cut out the foil.

**3** **Use tape to secure** the pattern to the top of the aluminum. With the foil side on the bottom, place on top of a piece of scrap wood or a thick pad of newspaper. Using an awl and a hammer, follow the dots on the pattern and punch holes through the paper and the aluminum. Use the hole punch to punch three larger holes along each edge as shown on the pattern.

**To make the candle covers you will need:**

Paper
Tracing paper
Scissors
Glass votive holder
Aluminum tooling foil (available at crafts stores)
Tape
Scrap piece of wood or thick pad of newspaper
Awl
Hammer
⅛-inch hole punch
Fine florist's wire
Silver sequins in sunburst or floral shapes
Household cement for metal (available at crafts, discount, hardware, and home center stores)

**4** **Remove the paper** pattern and gently role the aluminum into a cone, overlapping the edges slightly while lining up the ⅛-inch holes on each side. Use a piece of florist's wire, threaded through each set of ⅛-inch holes, to secure the edges of the tree together.

**5** **Glue sequins** to the outside surface of the cone, using the household cement.

*Note:* The candle heat will heat up the foil, so using a pot holder, lift the foil cone from the bottom edge rather than from the top when removing it from the glass holder. *Do not* leave the candle unattended. When storing the tree cones, stuff the inside with tissue to maintain the cone shape.

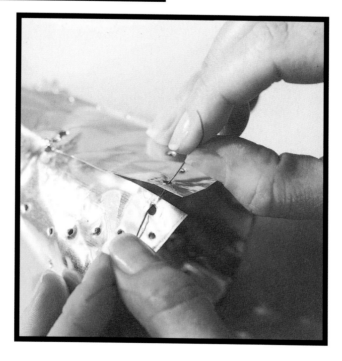

## 1 more idea...
● Experiment with your own punched designs, including stars and hearts.

## also try this...
● For a warm-weather version of this project, shape the foil into a cylinder and punch foil with holes in the shape of flowers.

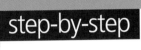

# silvery tree candle covers
(continued)

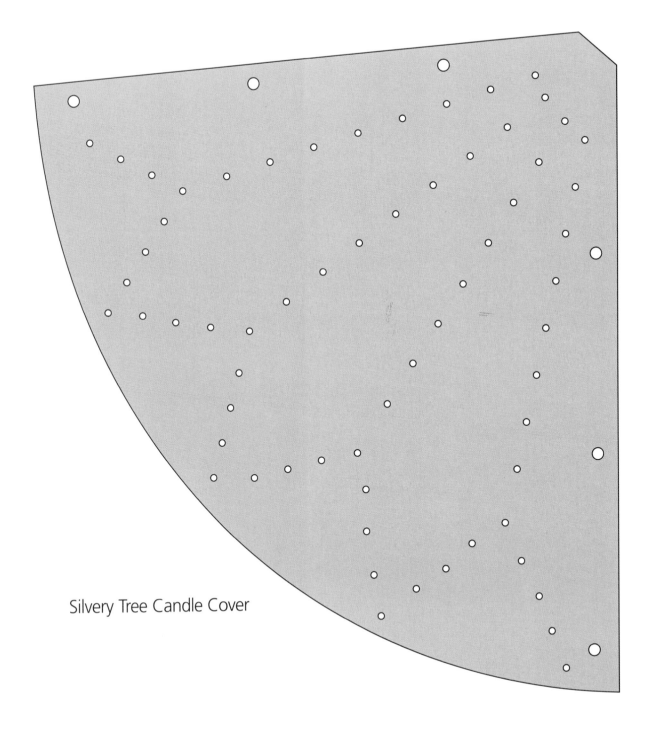

Silvery Tree Candle Cover

# snowy candle centerpiece

Make a snowy evening seem warm and cozy

by creating this winter centerpiece.

**To make the centerpiece you will need:**

Five clear glass ball ornaments

Five curtain rings (available at discount and home center stores)

Desired platter or plate

Epsom salt

Candles to fit into ornament openings

Assorted holiday greenery

**here's how** **Remove hangers** from ornaments. Arrange the curtain rings on the platter. Pour Epsom salt into each ornament, filling halfway to the top. Place the ornaments atop the curtain rings. Place candles into the openings of the ornaments, pressing into the Epsom salt to secure in place. Arrange holiday greenery around the candles as desired.

## 1 more idea...
- To add color to your arrangement, use colored sand instead of Epsom salt.

## also try this...
- For a large centerpiece, use pillar candles in rose bowls.

127

# good ideas *holiday presentations*

## Bowl them over

with the simplicity of presenting favorite holiday items piled high in beautiful bowls. Ribbon candy, winter-white tea candles, and tiny gift bows make striking and unexpected holiday presentations.

# more ideas *for* winter

❄ When you flip the calendar to December, light the way for visitors by placing luminaries along the front walkway or driveway.

❄ Pick up snowflake and snowmen pasta to celebrate the season during mealtimes together.

❄ Dress a snowman in an old knit hat and scarf, using mittens to cover his stick hands.

❄ Pick up some extra storage boxes to organize and store any new decorations or crafting supplies you've collected.

❄ To use next year, pick up sale-priced holiday items from party stores, such as napkins, serving platters, and goody boxes and bags.

❄ Save Christmas cards to decoupage gift boxes next holiday season.

* While holiday shopping, make a wish list of trims you'd like for the next year. After Christmas, revisit those items to see if you can buy them at a reduced price.

* Pick up pine-scented spray for an instant Christmas scent.

* Purchase a wreath and attach pre-made trims that can be enjoyed long after Christmas (such as snowmen, mittens, and snowflakes).

* Stock up on holiday fabrics when the after-Christmas sales begin.

* Fill a large clear cookie jar with fresh-from-the-oven gingerbread men cookies in all sizes.

* Use decorative scissors to trim portions of old Christmas cards to make gift tags.

*What would life be if we had*
*no courage to attempt anything?*

—— VINCENT VAN GOGH

*The freshness of spring* makes it even more fun to make new and clever gifts and decorations for your home. Gather your favorite crafting supplies and capture the beauty of spring.

spring

# springtime *scrapbook* cover

# Rickrack, ribbon, and glitter are all it takes to decoupage this springtime photo scrapbook cover.

**To make a scrapbook you will need:**
White acrylic paint (available at art, crafts, and discount stores)
Purchased vinyl covered photo scrapbook
Rickrack in desired colors
Ribbon in desired colors
Tacky glue
Royal Coat decoupage medium (available at crafts stores)
Iridescent glitter
Buttons, if desired

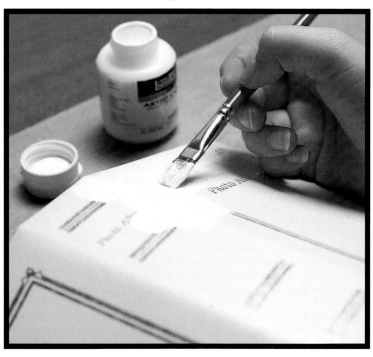

**Paint the scrapbook** with white paint. (*Note:* It may take two or three coats to cover the original scrapbook cover thoroughly.) Allow the paint to dry.

**1**

**2** **Arrange the rickrack** and ribbon on the cover overlapping the ends around the front and back covers. Use a dot of tacky glue to hold the trims in place. Using the decoupage medium, paint a coat under and over the rickrack and ribbon, coating the entire cover. Allow to dry. Apply a second coat and sprinkle with glitter. Glue on buttons, if desired.

## 1 more idea...
● Create a cheery sticker album for a child using this same technique on a sketch pad cover.

## also try this...
● Give this album to newlyweds, enclosing snapshots from the wedding ceremony.

# rose corsage vase

## A simple canning jar hides beneath
## this soft floral covering.

**To make the vase you will need:**
One yard of variegated deep pink ⅞-inch-wide wire-edged ribbon
Deep pink thread
Quart jar
Two 20-inch-diameter circles of organza or other sheer fabric in desired color
24 inches of 1½-inch-wide green wire-edged ribbon
Hot-glue gun and hot-glue sticks

**here's how** **To make the rose,** pull the wire out 2 to 3 inches on one end of the lighter-colored edge of the pink ribbon. Scrunch this end of the ribbon and wrap the wire around the edge to secure as shown in Diagram 1. Pull the wire on the same edge, from the opposite end of the ribbon. Pulling gently, evenly space gathers to a length of 12 inches. Scrunch the other end of the ribbon and wrap the wire around it. Cut off the excess wire.

Beginning with one end, roll the ribbon end 2 or 3 times. With coordinating thread, sew through the bottom edges to secure. Continue rolling the ribbon, moving the next layer slightly up from the bottom with each roll (see Diagram 2). As you roll, sew the edges to the prior layer. For ease in rolling and stitching, hold the rose upside down so the back side faces up. When near the end of the ribbon, fold the edge under (see Diagram 3) and stitch in place. Tie thread.

Gather the sheer fabric up around the jar evenly and tie at the top of the jar using green ribbon. Knot the green ribbon. Glue the ribbon rose over the knot in the green ribbon.

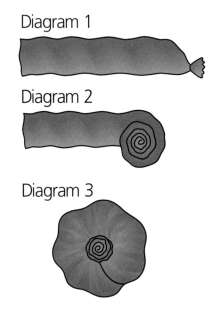

Diagram 1

Diagram 2

Diagram 3

## 1 more idea...
● For a quick candy holder, use a small bowl instead of a jar, adjusting the size of the fabric circle.

## also try this...
● This vase also makes an elegant container for paintbrushes and pencils or kitchen utensils.

# terrific tile *frames*

On your next trip to the home center store, pick up some ceramic tiles to make these fun frames.

**1** **Trim the photograph** as desired. Using spray photograph adhesive, spray the back of the photograph and center it on the mat board. The mat board can be trimmed, if desired, to allow only a narrow border of the mat board to show. Clean any overspray with a cotton ball and rubbing alcohol.

**2** **Position the mounted photograph** squarely onto the tile in the desired location. Use this as a guide for placing the bumpers. For the bottom two bumpers, clip a 90-degree corner out of each with scissors. (It doesn't have to be cut perfectly.) For the top two bumpers, cut them in half and place each as shown in the photograph, *left.* Placing the bumpers in this manner allows the photograph to be removed or replaced.

**3** **Remove the photograph** before decorating the tile. Be creative decorating the frame and bumper covers with the decorative trims, using the photograph, *opposite,* for inspiration. When applying a thin braid, dip and coat the entire piece in Mod Podge decoupage medium and position it as desired, cleaning off the excess Mod Podge with a damp cloth. Allow the Mod Podge to dry. If painting the tile, bake it in the oven if recommended by the manufacturer. Place the photograph in the frame and set it on an easel or attach an adhesive hanger to the back.

**To make a frame you will need:**

Scissors
Photograph
Spray photograph adhesive (available at art and crafts stores)
Colored mat board to coordinate with photograph, one inch larger on all sides than the photograph
Cotton ball
Rubbing alcohol
Desired tile
4 rubber, foam, or cork bumper pads (available at hardware stores)
Decorative trims such as braid, beads, gems, shells, and wood shapes
Mod Podge decoupage medium, if desired
Ceramic, glass, or tile paint (available at art and crafts stores)
Easel or adhesive hanger (available at crafts stores)

## 1 more idea...
● Frame a favorite pet photograph, trimming the tile with small treats coated in decoupage medium and an engraved pet tag.

## also try this...
● For the decorative trims, search hardware and business supply stores as well as crafts stores.

## good ideas *collections in glass*

A clear glass container becomes a clever way to unveil a favorite collection. Simply choose an appropriately-sized container and fill it with your prized pieces. Tie a fabric-strip gingham bow around the handle or the container top, and your collections are creatively displayed for all to enjoy.

# family photo wraps

**To make the photo wraps you will need:**
Family photographs
White mat board in desired size
Clear tape

Personalize the wrap as well as the gift with this lovingly created paper.

**here's how** **To make this project** arrange photographs on the white mat board, overlapping them as desired. Using small rings of tape, secure the backs of the photographs to the mat board. Take the photo-covered mat board to a copy center and photocopy the arrangement in black and white as many times as desired. *Note:* To make gift wrap for small packages, you may want to reduce the image size on the photocopies. Wrap the gifts as desired.

## 1 more idea...
● To make a colored wrap, choose color photographs and a coordinating color of mat board.

## also try this...
● For other personalized wrapping papers, try photocopying arrangements of badges, report cards, or nameplates.

# elegant towel holders

Make guests feel welcome by trimming their towels with glistening jewels.

**To make a towel holder you will need:**
One yard of craft wire
Approximately 1¼-inch-diameter tube, such as a plastic camera film holder, pill bottle, or spice container
Needle-nose pliers
Assorted beads

**here's how** **To make this project** wrap the wire around the tube. (*Note:* We used a plastic camera film holder.) Using the needle-nose pliers, twist one end of the wire to form a closed loop.

String beads from the opposite end of the wire. To make the pink napkin ring, put a heart bead as the first and last beads. Use alternate colors and sizes of beads to string onto the wire for a varied pattern that can be repeated.

String beads until you have four or five coils strung. After the last bead is on, use the needle-nose pliers, twisting the wire to form another closed loop. Cut off the excess wire.

## 1 more idea...
- Old necklaces, jewelry findings, shells, and buttons are also fun to string for this project.

## also try this...
- Use these beaded coils as elegant napkin rings.

# *mosaic* tile pot and frame

Once plain-Jane, this terra-cotta pot and old picture frame transform into striking accent pieces when embellished with broken pieces of shiny tile.

**1** **For the pot,** paint the inside of the pot with blue paint. For the frame, paint the outside edge and inside edge of the opening with white acrylic paint. Allow the paint to dry.

**2** **Place the tiles** on one end of the towel and fold the other end over the tiles. Hit the tiles with a hammer to break them into small pieces. *Note:* Do not break tiles uncovered without wearing safety glasses to protect your eyes.

**Determine the placement** of the tile **3** pieces on the frame or pot and glue in place, leaving space between the pieces for grout. Let the glue dry.

**4** **Mix grout with water** to a medium consistency in a plastic bowl. (*Note:* If you have to leave the project for a few minutes, cover the bowl with a lid to prevent the grout from drying out.) Use a knife to spread the grout over the surface of the project, filling all the cracks between the pieces.

**5** **Wipe off the excess grout** with a sponge or rag, then clean the surfaces with a damp rag. Let the grout dry.

## To make the mosaic projects you will need:
Paintbrush
Hammer
Old towel
Tacky glue
White grout (without sand)
Plastic bowl with lid
1-inch-wide putty knife
Sponge and rags

## To make the pot you will need:
Blue acrylic paint (available in art, crafts, and discount stores)
6- or 7-inch terra-cotta flower pot
3 white tiles (tiles available at home center stores)
3 yellow tiles
2 blue tiles

## To make the frame you will need:
White acrylic paint (available at art, crafts, and discount stores)
Frame with a 4×6-inch opening
3 white tiles

## 1 more idea...
● Bring new life to an old end table using this broken tile technique on the table top.

## also try this...
● Fill the pot with seed packages and garden tools for a spring gift.

# april showers tablecloth

Create a sheer organza table covering with springtime messages written on the borders.

**here's how** **To make this project** cut a 45-inch square from the fabric and four 6½×45-inch border strips, leaving the selvage edges on the ends of each strip. Sew a border strip to one side of the square cloth, using a ¼-inch seam allowance. Press the seam toward the border strip. Fold the other edge of the strip up over the seam and zigzag the edge to the seam. Repeat for the remaining three sides and three strips. (*Note:* The corners of each strip do not overlap.) Spray the border with fabric finish and press with an iron set on delicate.

Using a pen, write "April Showers–May Flowers" on the paper strip. Slip this strip under one of the borders and pin the fabric to the paper. With the gold pen and tracing the writing on the paper strip, transfer the lettering to the fabric. Repeat for each side.

Sew the cord of a tassel to each corner of the cloth. Sew a fabric flower over the top of the cord. Tack a single flower between the words "Shower" and "May."

## 2 more ideas...

● To make a personalized wedding or shower tablecloth, write the couple's names on the fabric edges.

● For a winter version of this tablecloth, write, "Let it Snow," "Joy to the World," or "Silent Night, Holy Night."

# spring-motif
## *etched glasses*

# Easy-to-do etching adds springtime motifs to clear and colored tumblers.

**1** **Clean glasses with hot water** and rinse with white vinegar. (*Note:* Avoid getting fingerprints on the areas to be etched.) Cut a piece of Contact paper 1 inch larger all around than the desired pattern on *page 150*.

**2** **Use carbon paper** to trace the pattern onto the Contact paper and cut out shapes using a crafts knife. Set the cut out portions aside and peel the backing from the remaining piece (negative portion or the piece with the hole left in it) of Contact paper and place it on the glass. Some of the edges might need to be clipped to enable the paper to lay flat. Burnish (rub down) all of the edges of the paper.

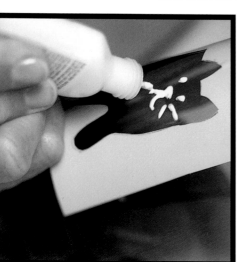

**3** **For the cat glass:** Use ¼-inch adhesive vinyl letters to spell "meow" inside the word balloon. Use the paint pen to add details to face. Allow the paint to dry several hours before etching.

**For the sunflower glass:** Use the paint pen to draw a center circle. Add a series of paint dots inside the circle for seeds. Draw petal divisions using the paint pen, using the pattern, *page 150*, as a guide.

**For the bee glass:** Follow the instructions in Step 1 and Step 2, *above*.

**4** **Wearing rubber gloves,** paint on the etching cream following the manufacturer's instructions. Allow to set and then rinse thoroughly.

**5** **Peel off** the Contact paper, paint, and/or letters. Wash the glass thoroughly before using.

## To make the etched glasses you will need:
Plain clear or colored glasses
White vinegar
Contact paper (available at discount and home center stores)
Carbon paper
Crafts knife
Spoon for burnishing
¼-inch adhesive vinyl letters
Fabric paint pen (available at art, crafts, discount, and fabric stores)
Rubber gloves
Etching cream
Paintbrush with natural bristles or a sponge brush

## 2 more ideas...
● Use vinyl letters to personalize your own glasses with the initial of your last name.

● Etch the name of each family member onto a glass—don't forget Grandma and Grandpa!

# spring-motif etched glasses
(continued)

Spring-Motif Etched Glasses

# beaded bobeche

A metal washer and an
## eclectic collection of beads
### combine to make a
## colorful fringed skirt
#### for a taper.

**To make the bobeche you will need:**
Metallic gold spray paint
Metal washer with a 7/8- to 1-inch opening
White quilting or beading thread
Beading needle
Silver glass seed beads
Assorted glass beads
Beacon Fabri Tac permanent adhesive (available at crafts and fabric stores)
Toothpick

here's how | **To make this project** spray paint the washer and let it dry.

Cut a 36-inch length of beading thread. Thread the needle. Tie a seed bead on one end of the thread to prevent the beads from slipping off.

Tie a knot in the thread 3 inches from the end and start beaded fringe, leaving ½ inch of thread between each string of beads. String the first row of beads, starting with the top bead. After the last bead of the fringe is strung, add a seed bead. (See Diagram 1.) Push the needle back up through the beads, starting with the bead above the seed bead and going back through the first bead. Repeat with the next row. *Note:* We used 14 fringes to make our bobeche, alternating 1¾- and 1¼-inch lengths. The longer fringes have matching heart beads on the bottom.

Apply a drop of adhesive to the back of the washer and glue on the first length of fringe. Apply glue to the edge of the washer and glue thread. The beads should be next to the washer edge as shown in Diagram 2. Use a toothpick to flatten the thread into the glue and to go back and put excess thread loops into the glue. Glue the fringe lengths around the edge of the washer, spacing the lengths approximately ⅓ inch apart. Cut off the excess ends of thread. Slip the bobeche over the taper so it rests on the candleholder.

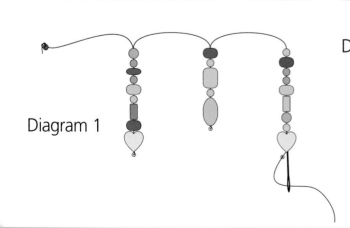

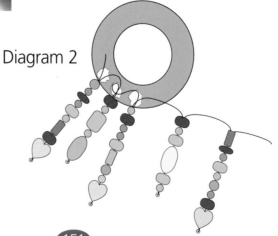

Diagram 2

Diagram 1

## 2 more ideas...

● For an unforgettable birthday cake, make mini versions of these bobeches to slip over the plastic candleholders.

● Use this beading technique to transform an ordinary chandelier into an extraordinary work of art.

# good ideas *springtime bottles*

A personalized message can be
preserved in glass forever, using the same
etching technique as shown on *page 149*.
Simply use small frame-shaped pieces of
Contact paper and adhesive-backed vinyl
letters to achieve this clever effect on
colored or clear bottles.

# memory box

Organize your treasured photos to enjoy at a moment's notice with a designer-style box that doubles as a handsome home accessory.

## To make the box you will need:

3 different kinds of papers, such as corrugated, art, and wrapping papers
Adhesive spray (available at art and crafts stores)
7½×11½-inch photo box
Crafts glue
½ yard of desired ribbon
Round-head paper fasteners (available at discount and office supply stores)
Awl
5×7-inch photo mat
Four #10 washers (available at hardware stores)
Photograph

**here's how** **To make this project** cut two strips of paper each measuring 5×19½ inches to cover the sides of the box. Spray the back of one strip with adhesive. Line the paper up with the top edge and one corner of the box and wrap the paper around one side and end. Fold the excess paper to the under side. Repeat with the second strip to cover the remaining side and end. If necessary, use glue to secure the edges.

Cut contrasting paper ¾ inch larger all around than the top. Spray the back of the paper with adhesive and center over the lid top. Fold the excess over the edge. From paper to be used on the rim, cut a 6×8-inch rectangle and glue to the center top of lid. Cut ribbon in half and glue one strip across each end of the paper, gluing the ends over the edge.

Cut a paper strip (we used corrugated paper) the circumference of the lid plus ¼ inch. Equally space and attach paper fasteners around the strip (eight on each side and five on each end). Apply crafts glue to the rim and wrap paper strip around rim. Overlap the extra ¼ inch around a corner.

Using an awl, punch a hole in each corner of the mat. Slip a washer over the ends of a paper fastener and slip through the hole, securing the ends of fastener to the back. Center and glue the edges of the photograph to the back of the mat. Glue the mat to the top of the paper-covered lid.

## 1 more idea...

• To keep your treasury of recipes at hand, choose papers that coordinate with your kitchen and turn this memory box into a lovely recipe file.

## also try this...

• Leftover wallpaper, fabric pieces, and heavy-weight tissue paper also make nice memory box coverings.

# pearl-edged lamp shade scarf

Make the lighting—and the lamp—
**soft and romantic** with this quick-to-make
lamp shade scarf.

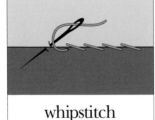

**To make the
lamp shade scarf
you will need:**
19×19-inch piece of
  lime green
  sparkling organdy
3 yards of pale pink
  pearl beaded string
  (available at crafts
  and fabric stores)
Pink sewing thread
Sewing needle

**here's how** **To make
this project**
fold a ¼-inch hem along each
side of the organdy and
press. Refold a second ¼-inch
hem to make a double hem
and press.

Beginning 2½ inches from
the end of beaded string,
whipstitch the string to the
corner of the scarf. Whipstitch
the string along one edge,
leaving a 2½-inch tail at the
next corner. Cut the string.
Repeat for each edge of
the scarf.

Cut four 2¾-inch lengths
of beaded string. Place one
of these strings at each
corner, centered between the
two beaded string tails. Stitch
in place.

*Caution:* Do not leave the
lamp unattended when the
light is on.

whipstitch

## 1 more idea...

● To dress up a child's
  lamp, stitch small game
  pieces or favorite charms
  to the scarf corners.

## also try this...

● These pretty scarves look
  lovely sitting beneath a
  collection of perfume
  bottles or elegantly
  framed photographs.

# good ideas *gift-of-money frames*

You could tuck a gift of money into a greeting card, but why do the expected? Fold and place the bill (or bills) in an elegant picture frame for a clever disguise. With a frame to keep and money to spend, this kind gesture will never be forgotten.

# good ideas *tulips in tumblers*

Glasses aren't just for drinking anymore. Vintage tumblers in all colors, textures, and sizes make interesting vessels to hold small spring bouquets. Group several together for a breathtaking floral display.

# easter sacks of goodies

Help the Easter Bunny
by filling these sacks of goodies
and hiding them on
Easter morning.

**To make the Easter sacks you will need:**
Pencil
Cookie cutters in desired shapes
Brightly colored sacks (available at paper, gift, or crafts stores)
Cardboard
Single-edge razor blade or X-Acto knife
Clear cellophane
Tape
Rickrack, if desired

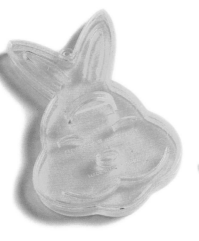

**here's how** **To make this project** draw around the cookie cutter on the front of the sack. Place a piece of cardboard between the layers of the sack. Using the single-edge razor blade or X-Acto knife, cut away the shape of the cookie cutter. Cut a piece of cellophane a little larger than the hole and tape it inside the sack. (*Note:* You can tape rickrack or other trims on top of the cellophane before taping it to the sack, if desired.) Fill the sack with popcorn or other goodies.

## 1 more idea...
● To wrap your homemade jams and jellies, cut fruit shapes out of the bag and tuck your kitchen treats inside.

## also try this...
● Check stores for colored cellophane to brighten up your gift bags.

A single piece of jewelry or a mini-grouping of game pieces glued to a piece of ribbon make fun napkin rings. Guests will be delighted with your clever tabletop, especially if they can keep their napkin ring as a gift from you.

# good ideas *clever napkin rings*

make it in minutes

# wooden frames

Add pizzazz to everyday wood frames by simply adding painted wooden doodads.

**To make the wooden frames you will need:**

Small wood frames
Assorted wood cutouts and shapes such as, stars, hearts, and small finials for a dollhouse (available at crafts stores)
Acrylic paints in desired colors
Small paintbrush
Hot-glue gun and hot-glue sticks

## 1 more idea...

● Instead of a photograph, frame a mirror and embellish it with wood pieces for a unique looking glass.

## also try this...

● Search drawers for mini embellishments for your frames, such as buttons and single earrings.

**here's how** **To make this project** paint the frame and the small wood cutouts and/or shapes as desired. Allow the paint to dry thoroughly. Using hot glue, attach the pieces to the frame using the photograph, *above,* for ideas.

# see-through-it plate and goblet

You'll make a great impression

when you serve guests from these

jeweled beauties.

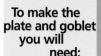

**To make the plate and goblet you will need:**

Clear glass plate and goblet

Glass luster gems (usually used in flower vases, available at crafts, discount, and floral shops)

Glue used for glass

**here's how** **To make this project**
wash the plate and goblet in hot, soapy water. Allow to dry thoroughly. Working in a well-ventilated room and following the directions on the glue, glue the gems in place. (*Note:* You may want to let the glue set up for two or three minutes before placing the gem on so it doesn't slip.) Allow the glue to dry thoroughly. When necessary, handwash the items carefully.

## 1 more idea...
● Add sparkle to vases, candleholders, candy dishes, and more, using these beautiful colored gems.

## also try this...
● For a grand wedding gift, make the couple a set of glasses using gems in the same color scheme as used in their wedding.

# beaded
## *tassels*

# Make these ornate designer tassels

## with just a few supplies and at a fraction of the cost.

**1** Cut a 10-inch length of beading thread to use for the tassel hanger. Tie a knot near one end and string 5 inches of seed beads onto the thread, knotting the other end. Tape the beaded length to a long (top) edge of the cardboard. Cut a 24-inch length of pearl cotton to use later for the wrap.

Tape one end of the pearl cotton skein to the bottom edge of the cardboard. Wrap the pearl cotton around the 4-inch cardboard width, winding evenly and close together. Tape the end to the bottom.

**4** Cut a 36-inch length of beading thread and thread needle. Tie a seed bead on one end of the thread, and trim off the excess tail. Put the needle through the inside of the tassel top and come out below the bottom edge of the wrap. The bead will catch in the tassel top and secure the thread.

**2** Wrap the metallic braid on top of the pearl cotton, taping the ends as before. Push the fibers to the center of the cardboard.

Remove the tape from the beaded length. Tie tightly at the top, knotting to secure. Trim the ends and slide the knot underneath the wrapped threads.

**5** String beads the length of the tassel in a desired pattern, ending with 3 seed beads. Go back through the beads, starting with the fourth from the bottom. The first three beads will form a tiny loop. When the top is reached, pull the thread to remove any slack. Go back through the tassel under the bottom of the wrap. Come above the wrap, then carry the needle back to the bottom of the wrap, coming out ⅛ inch from the prior fringe beading. Continue making beaded fringe around the entire tassel. End thread by going through inside tassel top a few times to secure.

**3** Using scissors, carefully cut a small rectangle from the side of the cardboard as shown, *above*.

Using the 24-inch length of pearl cotton previously cut for the wrap, make a loop and hold the short end (A) in place with finger. Wrap the other end (B) around the tassel, ½ inch down from the tassel top. Wrap tight and close together. When wrapping is completed, thread the B end through the loop and trim the B end to ½ inch. Pull the A end until the loop pulls the B end under the wrapping. Cut off excess A end.

**To make the tassels you will need:**
Sharp scissors
1 skein DMC #3 pearl cotton in desired color (pearl cotton and braid available at crafts, fabric, and needlework stores)
Glass seed beads in desired color (beads available at crafts, discount, and needlework stores)
Tape
4×6-inch piece of lightweight cardboard
1 spool Kreinik metallic #8 braid in desired color
White beading thread (available at crafts stores)
Beading needle
Small bugle beads in desired color

## 1 more idea...
- For a fun Christmastime tassel, add a tiny jingle bell to the bottom of each beaded fringe.

## also try this...
- Use these gorgeous tassels for ornamentation on pillows, curtains, and table coverings.

**make it in minutes**

# rose-topped eggs

A simple
floral touch turns an
ordinary dyed egg
into an elegant
springtime
decoration.

**To make the rose-topped eggs you will need:**
Hardboiled or blown-out eggs
Commercial egg dye or food coloring
Tacky glue
Miniature dried rose buds (available at crafts or discount stores)
Glass candleholders

**here's how** **To make this project** dye eggs using egg dye or food coloring. Allow to dry thoroughly. Spread tacky glue around the smallest end of the egg. Arrange five or six dried buds on the top of the egg and allow to dry. To display the eggs, place them in a variety of glass candleholders.

## 2 more ideas...

● Some potpourri contains lovely shapes of dried flowers that also can be used for this project.

● To hang these lovely eggs, simply glue a small ribbon to the end of the egg before adding the roses.

# embellished porcelain knobs

Turn any piece of furniture into a showpiece by replacing the pulls with these hand-painted originals.

**To make the painted knobs you will need:**

Purchased porcelain drawer pulls in desired sizes

Liquitex Glossies paint (available at art and crafts stores)

**here's how** **To make this project**

paint the porcelain drawer pulls using the desired designs and paint colors, referring to the photograph, *right*, for ideas. To heat-set the colors to be permanent, bake the knobs in the oven following the manufacturer's directions.

## 1 more idea...

● This painting technique can be used to dress up other porcelain and glass items such as canisters, cookie jars, and toothbrush holders.

## also try this...

● To make a perfect dot, dip the handle tip of a small paintbrush into the paint and dab onto the surface to be painted.

# yards-of-beads candleholders

Purchased by the yard, these strings of elegant pearls wrap around glass votive holders and secure in place with tiny dots of glue.

**To make the candleholders you will need:**
Tacky glue
Glass votive candleholder
Approximately 2 yards of beads by the yard (available at crafts and fabric stores)
Votive candle

 **here's how** **To make this project**
place a dot of glue at the bottom edge of the votive candleholder and press one end of the beaded string to the glue. When secure, wrap the beaded string around the candleholder, securing every inch or so with glue. Wrap to desired spot, cut string, and secure end with glue. Insert candle into holder.

## 1 more idea...
- Wrap perfume bottles in the same manner for an extraordinary display.

## also try this...
- Group the candleholders on a clear plate to create a stunning centerpiece.

happy *easter* eggs

# Decorate a basket of eggs

### in no time with findings from the kitchen drawer.

**To make the eggs you will need:**
Hardboiled or blown-out eggs
Commercial egg dye or food coloring
Star stickers (available at crafts, discount, and office supply stores)
Rubber bands

1 **Prepare the egg dye** as instructed on the package or use food coloring to dye the eggs.

2 **To make the star eggs,** press the star stickers on the eggs. Rub carefully around the edges of the stickers. Dip the eggs in the dye. Remove the stickers.

3 **To make the striped eggs,** wrap rubber bands around the eggs, using wide rubber bands or combining more than one rubber band. Dip the eggs in the dye. Remove the rubber bands.

## 1 more idea...
● If you don't have time to dye the eggs, simply wrap them with brightly colored rubber bands for a whimsical look.

## also try this...
● Try using circle reinforcements as stickers to create circle shapes on the eggs.

# jelly bean pots

**Perfect for** Easter, May Day, or Mother's Day, **these treats will bring** sweet smiles.

**To make the jelly bean pots you will need:**
Small terra-cotta flower pots
Acrylic paint in desired colors (available at art, crafts, and discount stores)
Paintbrush
Sandpaper
Colored Easter grass, shredded mylar, or tissue paper
Candy

**here's how** **To make this project** paint the flower pots with a desired color of acrylic paint. If you wish, you can use more than one color of paint on the pot or paint designs on the pot. Let the paint dry thoroughly.

Sand the edges of the pot to remove some of the paint. This will give the pot an antique look.

Fill the pots with Easter grass, shredded mylar, or tissue paper. To complete the treat holder, fill it with candy.

## 1 more idea...
● To use these rustic pots as a fun centerpiece, group and stack several painted pots in the center of the table, filling each with dried flowers.

## also try this...
● When the holiday is over, use these clever pots for holding pencils and crayons, or straws and plastic forks and spoons for a party.

# more ideas *for* spring

- Fill a pair of bright rubber boots with sand and add a pretty umbrella as a decorative welcome on the front porch.

- When doing spring cleaning, organize crafting supplies in see-through plastic containers with snap-on lids.

- Replace your wintertime candles with the cheerful hues of spring.

- Put out springtime welcome mats by the front and back doors.

- Place pastel-colored candies in candy dishes, small bowls, or clear jars.

- Poke an artificial flower or two into your indoor plants.

- Search garage sales for odds and ends of china and pottery to break and use for mosaic projects.

- Put out handsoaps with fragrant floral scents.

- Wrap guest towels with a garland made from artificial flowers and ivy.

- Touch up your outdoor pots with some easy-to-do painting techniques.

- To hardboil eggs without cracking, place eggs in cold water before turning on the burner.

- Save your seed packets to use in a decoupage project (see *pages 204–205*).

- Freshen up couches and chairs by using spring-colored pillows and throws.

*Nothing in the world is so powerful*
*as an idea whose time has come.*

—— VICTOR HUGO

# summer

The relaxing days of summer are perfect days for creating quick projects that light up the season. Bring the warmth of summer's sun indoors with these easy-to-do ideas you'll be proud to display or give to someone close at heart.

# folk art fruit coasters

The beauty of the fruit of the season is easy to duplicate with a little fabric and simple running stitches.

Apple Coaster

**here's how** **To make this project** trace the patterns on *page 183* onto tracing paper and cut out. Cut two 4-inch squares of light tan fabric for each coaster, one to be stitched for the top and one left unstitched for the back. Use patterns to cut two leaves from green fabric for each coaster. Cut pear shape from dark yellow fabric, orange from orange fabric, and apple from red fabric. Cut one 3½-inch square of batting for each coaster.

Arrange a fruit shape and two leaves on a light tan fabric square, the fruit overlapping the bottom ends of the leaves. Pin the pieces in place. Using a running stitch (see diagram on *page 183*), stitch around the inside edges of the fruit and leaves ⅛ inch from the edge. Repeat for each fruit coaster top.

Center a batting square on top of a fabric back, then center the stitched fruit square on top of the batting. Pin the three layers together. Stitch around the outside edges of the fruit and leaves, ⅛ inch from the edge, using a running stitch and stitching through all three layers (see drawings, *left*, and on *page 182*). Keeping edges aligned, stitch around the outside, ¼ inch from the edge.

Mix textile medium with lime green paint. Paint highlights on each fruit shape, allowing brushstrokes to show on each end.

### To make the coasters you will need:

Tracing paper
Scissors
¼ yard of light tan fabric
Scraps of green, dark yellow, orange, and red fabrics
Quilt batting (available at crafts, discount, and fabric stores)
Straight pins
Light tan DMC quilting thread
Sewing needle
Lime green acrylic paint
Aleene's Enhancers Textile Medium (available at crafts stores)
Paintbrush

## 1 more idea...

● To make a striking table runner, cut these fruit patterns from felt and appliqué to a large felt rectangle.

## also try this...

● Add these fresh designs to your kitchen by sewing the fabric shapes onto curtains, hot pads, and tablecloths.

# folk art fruit coasters
(continued)

Orange Coaster

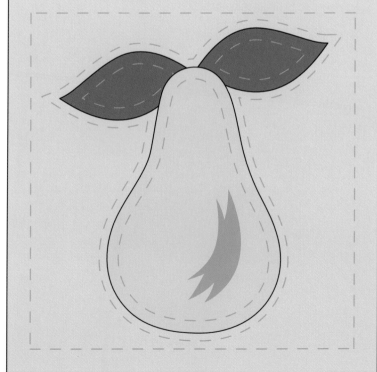

Pear Coaster

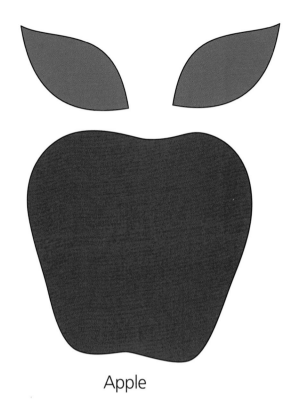

Apple

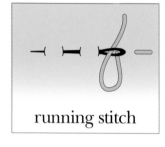

running stitch

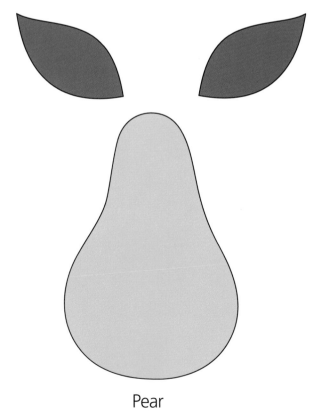

Pear

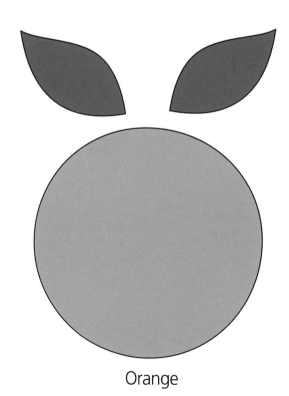

Orange

# licorice pots

Any sweet tooth will be happy with these clever pots filled with colorful licorice.

**To make the pots you will need:**
Terra-cotta pot (we used a 6-inch pot)
Large rickrack
Buttons
Tacky glue
Acrylic paint in desired color
Paintbrush
Clear cellophane or plastic wrap
Licorice or other candy

**here's how** **To make this project**
glue rickrack around the lip of the pot and allow the glue to dry. Glue buttons atop the rickrack as desired.

Paint vertical stripes or squiggles on the pot. Let the paint dry. Cut a large square of cellophane or clear plastic wrap and put inside the pot. Fill the pot with licorice or other candy.

## 1 more idea...
● For a quicker decorated pot, use stickers and labels instead of buttons, rickrack, and acrylic paint.

## also try this...
● For a friend who feels under the weather, fill the pot with tea bags, cocoa mix, bath oil, or good reading material.

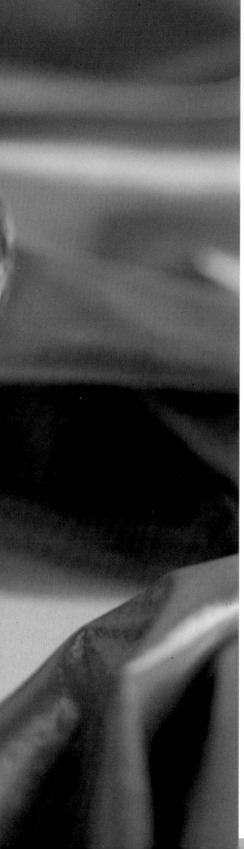

# lacey bottles

Snippets of lace and clear bottles all come together to make these elegant glass containers.

**To make the bottles you will need:**
Assorted bottles or small flower vases
Lace motifs and trims as desired to fit bottles (available at crafts, discount, and fabric stores)
Mod Podge decoupage medium
Small paintbrush

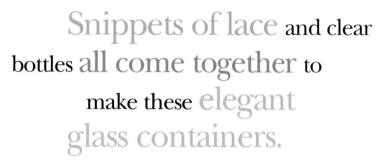

**here's how** **To make this project** arrange the lace on the bottle until you have a pleasing arrangement. When using a length of trim, cut out some of the connecting threads so the points can be spread out to fit the curvature of the bottle if necessary.

With the paintbrush, spread some Mod Podge on the bottle in the general shape of the trim. Put the lace in place and cover it thoroughly with Mod Podge. Allow to dry.

## 1 more idea...
- To give the lace a vintage look, soak it in tea and let it dry before gluing it to the bottle.

## also try this...
- Use small premade crocheted doilies to dress up glassware.

# good ideas *frame a book*

Preserve that special child's book by framing it to hang on the wall. Choose books that are fairly flat and frame them yourself, or take any book to your local frame shop and they can adjust the depth of the frame.

# doily note cards

Tiny doily scraps and little bits of ribbon make plain writing paper beautifully fancy.

**To make the note cards you will need:**

Scraps of paper such as parchment, watercolor, craft, or scrapbook
Decorative-edged scissors, if desired
Assorted doilies
Crafts glue
Paper punch and thin ribbon, if desired

## 1 more idea...
● To color white doilies, simply spray with a light dusting of spray paint.

## also try this...
● To tie these dainty cards to a gift bag or package, simply punch a hole in the corner of the card near the fold and thread with a piece of narrow ribbon or cording.

here's how **To make this project** cut the paper in the desired card size (when open) and fold it in half. Trim the edges using decorative-edged scissors, if desired. Trim the doily if necessary to fit the front of the note card. Glue the doily in place. If desired, trim the note card with small pieces of ribbon, using a paper punch to make holes to insert the ribbon.

# beaded bookmarks

## You'll never want to put that book down when it carries your favorite colorful bookmark.

**here's how** **To make the fuchsia bookmark** tie a knot 1 inch from the end of the ribbon. Slide bead (or beads) from the opposite end of the ribbon up to the knot. Tie a knot on the other side of the bead(s) to hold in place.

For the other end of the bookmark, measure 10 inches from the inside knot and tie another knot. Put on the bead(s) and slide up to the knot. Tie another knot against the last bead. Trim the ribbon ends.

**To make the fringed bookmark,** tie a knot on one end of the ribbon and trim the end close to the knot. Thread the beading needle and go through the ribbon knot to secure the end of the thread in the knot. String on 19 multi-colored rocaille beads, then 4 silver seed beads. Take the needle back through the rocaille beads. The seed beads will form a loop at the end. Go back through the ribbon knot, pulling the thread so the fringe hangs below the knot. Repeat with another string of fringe. Make 5 strings. Secure the end of the thread in the knot.

Slide on a silver bead from the other end of the ribbon and pull over the ribbon knot holding the fringe. Tie a knot against the bead to hold it in place. For the other end of the bookmark, measure 10 inches from this knot and tie another knot. Slide on a silver bead and tie a knot on the other side of the bead to secure. Trim the end of the ribbon.

### To make the bookmarks you will need:

17 inches of ⅜-inch-wide double-faced satin ribbon for each bookmark
Beads with large openings (available at crafts and discount stores)

**For the fuchsia bookmark:**
3 clear blue faceted beads and 1 white frosted bead

**For the blue fringed bookmark:**
2 silver beads, multi-colored silver-lined large rocaille beads, and silver seed beads
Beading needle
White beading thread

## 2 more ideas...

- To personalize a bookmark, write a name on the ribbon using a permanent marker.

- Make both beaded ends the same and use your ribbon as a gift tie to cinch up a surprise sack.

Purchased plain bottles are
dressed up in a hurry
then filled with
vinegar, oil, or
other special
goodies.

# dressed-up bottles

**here's how** **To make the paper embellished bottle,** layer desired strips of corrugated cardboard and papers around the bottle and tie with raffia. Glue two artificial leaves and an anise pod to the front of the paper strips.

**To make the beaded bottle,** cut a 24-inch length of copper wire. Randomly wrap and twist wire around the bottle adding beads as desired.

**To make the vinegar bottle,** use a Deco Color pen to write "Vinegar" on the side of the bottle. Group and tie berries and herbs onto a small plastic ring and slip around the neck of the bottle.

## To make the bottles you will need:

Tall decorative bottles (available at crafts and decorative home stores)
Hot-glue gun and hot-glue sticks

### For the paper embellished bottle:

Corrugated cardboard
Decorative paper
Natural raffia
Two artificial leaves
Anise pod

### For the beaded bottle:

18-gauge copper wire
Assorted beads

### For the vinegar bottle:

Deco Color pen in desired color (available at art and crafts stores)
Herbs
Red berries
Plastic ring to sit on bottle neck

## 1 more idea...

● Trim a pretty vessel with shells and fill with bath oil to display next to the bathtub.

## also try this...

● Tie a simple bow around the neck of the bottle and add a single flower.

*thank-you* note

# Make your
## thank you even more special
### by making the card yourself.

**To make the thank-you notes you will need:**
Tracing paper
Paper clips
Blank note card with matching envelope
Cutting board or old magazine
T-pin

**1** **Trace the words** "Thank You," *below*, onto tracing paper.

**2** **Turn the tracing paper** over (the words will be backwards) and clip it to the back side of the note card. Place the card and tracing paper on a cutting board or old magazine.

**3** **Using a T-pin,** evenly pierce holes along the written lines, piercing through the tracing paper and the card. Remove the tracing paper and turn the card over. Pierce holes along the edge of the envelope flap, if desired.

## 2 more ideas...

● Use this piercing technique to add your name or initials to the top of plain stationery.

● For an unforgettable wedding gift, personalize a set of note cards for the newlyweds by piercing their last name on the card fronts.

# painted candleholders

With just a little bit of paint, tiny strokes of color make plain candleholders works of art.

**To make the candleholders you will need:**
Glass candleholders
Deco Color paint pens in desired colors and widths (available at art and crafts stores)
Paint thinner, if desired

**here's how** **To make this project** wash the candleholders in hot soapy water. Allow them to dry thoroughly. Working in a well-ventilated room and using the photographs for ideas, begin to decorate the candleholder. Apply one color at a time and allow it to dry before adding other colors. *Note:* If you make a mistake, you can remove it with paint thinner.

## 2 more ideas...
- Revive an old candy jar using these user-friendly pens.

- To make a plaid design, first draw some horizontal stripes, then vertical stripes, then more horizontal stripes, letting the paint dry between the coats.

# nature lover's sponged pot

Every green thumb will appreciate this simple sponged flower pot.

**To make the sponged pot you will need:**

Terra-cotta pot (we used a 6½-inch pot)
Paintbrush
Green gloss acrylic paint (available at art, crafts, and discount stores)
White gloss acrylic paint
Tracing paper
Scissors
Thin sponge (available at discount stores)

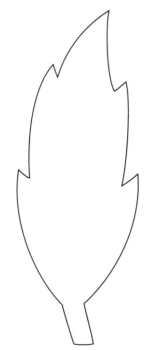

## 1 more idea...

● Bring nature indoors by sponging these leaves on a wall using flat acrylic or latex paint.

## also try this...

● Try other sponge shapes including suns, stars, and crescent moons.

**here's how** **To make this project** paint the inside of the pot using green paint. Let dry thoroughly. Paint the rim white and let dry.

Trace the leaf patterns onto tracing paper and cut out. Trace each leaf shape onto the sponge. Carefully cut out the leaf shapes using scissors.

Wet the sponges with water and wring out. To sponge the bottom, dip the large leaf shape into the green paint and press to the surface of the pot. Continue this procedure until desired number of leaves are painted. Sponge paint the rim of the pot using green paint and the small leaf sponge.

# simple celebrate plate

### Write a message for a special occasion on a clear plate and celebrate in style.

**To make the plate you will need:**
Tracing paper
Clear glass
  cake plate
Scissors
White vinegar
Tape
Paint pens in desired
  colors (usually
  used for fabric,
  available at art,
  crafts, and
  discount stores)

**here's how** **To make this project** trace around the outside edge of the plate onto the tracing paper and cut out. Draw a smaller circle inside the paper pattern to indicate the plate rim. Write "CELEBRATE" or any desired message within the rim area indicated on the tracing paper.

Wash the plate with hot water and rinse with white vinegar to remove any fingerprints. Let the plate dry completely. Tape the paper pattern with the message on top of the plate, right side up. Turn the plate upside down. The message can be seen, backwards, through the tracing paper. Use the fabric paint pens to write the message on the back side of the plate, following the pencil lines on the pattern.

Allow the paint to dry overnight. Remove the pattern and turn the plate over. (*Note:* The back of the plate is *not* washable, but it can be reused if the front is wiped or carefully rinsed.) To write a new message, simply peel the paint off the back of the plate.

## 2 more ideas...

● A single candy jar works for every season by simply changing the message or design using paint pens in the colors of the season.

● For a small dinner gathering, personalize clear glass chargers or water goblets with each guest's name.

dad's *garden gift*

Made with sun-catching jewels and sturdy cement, this stepping stone is sure to be a favorite in the garden.

**To make the stone you will need:**

Alphabet cookie cutters
Water-based paint, any color
Paper the size of stepping stone
Cement containing gravel and sand
Disposable plastic planter tray
Trowel or short length of lumber
Colored aquarium gravel
Flat decorative marbles
Glitter

**1** **Plan out decoration** arrangement before beginning. To test layout of lettering, dip cookie cutters in water-based paint and stamp onto paper.

**2** **Mix the cement** according to the instructions on the package. Pour the cement into a molding container such as a plastic planter pan. Shake side to side and tap sides of pan to settle cement into container. Smooth off the surface with a trowel or short length of lumber.

**Decorate the wet cement** **3** with colored aquarium gravel and flat marbles as desired. Press firmly into the cement. Excess cement can be washed off later.

**4** **Allow the cement** to settle but not harden before imprinting letters. Check occasionally to see if a clean imprint can be achieved. This may take up to an hour or a little more. A sharp imprint will not be achieved if the cement is imprinted too early. Just trowel again and continue to watch until the cement is at the right stage. Water will probably continue to rise to the top of the cement. To remove the water, carefully place a paper towel flat on the top and lift away or use a hair dryer. After imprinting letters, sprinkle with glitter if desired.

## 1 more idea...

● For other stepping-stone trims, try placing coins, buttons, or old fishing lures (no hooks!) into the cement.

## also try this...

● Have all family members make their own stones and place near the edge of the garden.

# summertime *bows*

# Here's a new twist on bow making—just in time for summer gift-giving.

**To make the summer bows you will need:**
¾ yard of 2½-inch-wide ribbon
Scissors
Clothespin
Pipe cleaner
Desired decorative trims for bow centers, such as artificial flowers, birds, butterflies, wired pearl beads, costume jewelry, and buttons

**1** **Cut four ribbons** 6 inches long. Fold the ribbon in half lengthwise with the right sides facing and trim the ends to a point.

**2** **Fold the edges back** to meet the fold (in an accordion-like manner). Hold the pleat in place with a clothespin at the center.

**3** **Fold the remaining ribbons** in the same manner, adding each to the clothespin.

**4** **Remove the clothespin** and wrap the ribbon centers with a pipe cleaner to secure. Add purchased trims to bow centers as desired.

## 1 more idea...
● Give a large pillar candle extra reason to shine by trimming the base with one of these colorful bows.

## also try this...
● Glue a tiny photograph to the center of the bow for a personal touch.

# decoupage
## *flower pot*

# Seed packets are the inspiration for this bright and cheery flower pot.

**1** **Cut out the seed packet fronts,** emptying the seeds into separate labeled plastic bags, if necessary. Trim the edges of the seed packets with decorative-edged scissors, if desired.

**2** **Arrange the seed packets** on the pot, overlapping and cutting tops and bottoms as needed. Paint back of seed packets with the decoupage medium and press to the surface of the pot. When all of the packets are attached to the pot, coat the entire outside of the pot with decoupage medium and let dry.

**Attach sunflower seeds, 3** arranged like flower petals, onto the pot as desired using decoupage medium as the glue. When dry, give the entire outside of the pot one more coat of decoupage medium. Allow to dry.

## 1 more idea...
● Try this same technique using postcards, old stamps, or pieces cut from greeting cards.

## also try this...
● This decoupaged flower pot does double duty as a holder for garden markers, seed packets, or small hand tools.

# patriotic silverware

**To make the silverware you will need:**

Purchased flatware with white plastic handles

¼-inch-wide masking tape

Binder reinforcements (available at discount and office supply stores)

Deco Color paint pens (available at art and crafts stores)

Celebrate the red, white, and blue with a family picnic and our patriotic silverware.

## 1 more idea...

• Use small vinyl lettering to write initials or a short message on the flatware handles.

## also try this...

• For Christmas flatware, use red, green, and metallic silver and gold paints.

**here's how** **To make this project** wash the flatware with soap and water. Allow to dry thoroughly. Do not touch the handles.

To make stripes, wrap pieces of masking tape around the handles. Burnish (rub) the edges. To make circles, apply binder reinforcements as desired.

Paint the exposed portion with paint pens, stroking the paint in one direction. Allow the paint to dry thoroughly. Remove the masking tape or reinforcements. Make any necessary corrections using the paint pens.

*Note:* This flatware can be handwashed only.

# good ideas *fourth of july display*

Layer the colors of
Independence Day in
country milk bottles for a fun
and festive summer display.
These holiday treats are
ready to share—and they
store easily by covering
the top with plastic
wrap, secured with
a rubber band.

# summer teacup candles

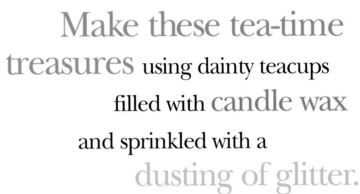

Make these tea-time treasures using dainty teacups filled with candle wax and sprinkled with a dusting of glitter.

**To make the teacup candles you will need:**
Small china teacups
Candle wax
Empty coffee can
Coloring for wax
    or old candles,
    if desired
White birthday
    candles
White glitter

**here's how** **To make this project** put hot water into the teacups to warm them as the wax is melting. Melt the wax in a coffee can setting the can in a pan of water on the stove or hot plate. (See the instructions for melting wax in the fall section, *page 35*.)

Color the wax using old colored candles, or purchased candle coloring, if desired. Remove the wax from the heat. Pour the hot water out of the cups and dry thoroughly. Carefully pour the wax into the cups and let them set until a soft covering appears on top of the wax (about two or three minutes). Push a birthday candle into the wax and steady it until it stands up straight. Add glitter to the top of the wax. *Note:* After the candle is completely burned, the cup can be washed in very hot water to remove the wax residue.

## 2 more ideas...

● For other great candle containers, scout flea markets for lone sugar jars, creamers, and small serving bowls.

● To add a decorative spoon to your teacup candle simply lay it on the saucer, securing with a dab of hot wax.

Chrysanthemum Chrysanthemum
Chrysanthemum
Chrysanth
Chrysanth
Chrysanth
cheerfulness
anthemum
themum

Red Rose Red Rose
Red Rose Red Rose
Red Rose
Red Rose
Love
Rose

Geranium Geranium
Geranium Geranium Ger
Geranium Ger
Geranium
preference
Geranium
Geranium

Violet Violet Violet
Violet Violet
Violet
Faithfulness
Violet

# good ideas *language of flowers gifts*

You can make your floral gifts even more special by attaching a tag that tells the real meaning of the flower you are giving. The Victorians called it the "language of flowers" and took the meaning behind each floral bouquet to heart. For a list of flowers and their meanings, just ask your local florist or your librarian.

# more ideas *for* summer

- At the end of June, tie a big red, white, and blue bow around your mailbox to celebrate Independence Day.

- Spend the day at the beach and bring along watercolor painting supplies.

- Just before blooms are about to fall, pick them and float them in water to enjoy for a few days longer.

- Buy terra-cotta pots to use all year long in crafting projects.

- Watch flea markets for china cups and cut glass tumblers to hold miniature floral bouquets.

- Pick up summertime crafting items such as shells, artificial flowers and berries, and bright-colored ribbons to create things on cold winter days.

✳ Clip out decorating and remodeling ideas from magazines for inspiration when the winter weather hits.

✳ Press fallen blooms to frame and enjoy all year long.

✳ Fill an old watering can with a colorful bouquet for a casual floral arrangement.

✳ Before tossing any worn-out clothing, clip the buttons off for use in crafting.

✳ Watch fabric-store sales for good buys on lightweight summertime fabrics to use in decorating.

✳ Make a seaside centerpiece using a sand pail, small shovel, sand, and interesting shells.

# glossary

**Aluminum tooling foil** – a thin aluminum sheet that can be easily pierced and bent for use in crafting

**Awl** – a pointed tool for marking surfaces or piercing small holes

**Battenburg** – named after Prince Henry of Battenburg, this lace is made in Belgium and is sometimes called Belgium lace or Brussels lace

**Batting** – layers or sheets of raw cotton, wool, or polyester used for lining quilts or for stuffing items such as pillows or dolls

**Beeswax** – a dull yellow when warm, this substance is secreted by bees and is used by the bee for constructing the honeycomb

**Beveled mirrors** – mirrors that have slanting angles to them

**Bugle bead** – a small cylindrical bead made of glass or plastic that is used for trimming, especially on women's clothing

**Burnish** – rub; to make shiny or lustrous by rubbing; polishing

**Chandelier prism** – a shaped decorative glass crystal from an ornate lighting fixture suspended from the ceiling

**Clear acrylic spray** – a clear spray used as a coating to protect surfaces

**Confetti** – small bits of brightly colored paper made for throwing (as at weddings)

**Cording** – a long slender flexible material usually consisting of several strands (as of thread or yarn) woven or twisted together

**Corsage bag** – a clear, plastic bag used as a package for an arrangement of flowers worn as a fashion accessory (can be found at floral shops)

**Corsage pin** – a straight pin with a head on it used for securing an arrangement of flowers worn on clothing as a fashion accessory

**Couscous pasta** – also called *Acini de Pepe,* this pasta is very tiny, like snippets of spaghetti

**Decorative-edge scissors** – scissors that have shaped blades that create a pattern when used, such as scallops and zigzags

**Decoupage** – the art of decorating surfaces by applying cutouts (as of paper) and then coating with several layers of finish

**Dowel** – a round rod or stick used for woodworking

**Enamel** – to beautify with a colorful surface; to form a glossy surface on

**Epsom salt** – a bitter colorless or white crystalline salt

**Etching cream** – an acid cream used to frost glass

**Fiberfill** – synthetic fibers used as a filling material (as for cushions)

**Finial** – usually a foliated ornament forming an upper extremity especially in Gothic architecture; a crowning ornament or detail (as a decorative knob)

**Floral oasis foam** – a green foam that is used to keep flowers in place when put into arrangements; available at crafts and floral stores

**Fusible webbing** – a strong, narrow, closely woven tape that can be bonded to something when heated (usually with an iron)

**Gingham** – a checkered fabric usually of yarn-dyed cotton in plain weave; striped cloth

**Grapevine wreath** – branches or twigs intertwined into a circular shape

**Grout** – a thin mortar used for filling spaces; any of various other materials (as a mixture of cement and water used for a similar purpose)

**Hot-glue** – solid sticks of glue that melt when inserted into a hot-glue gun

**Hot-glue gun** – a hand-held crafting tool that melts glue sticks and has a trigger-controlled grip to release melted glue from the tip of the gun

**Metallic papers** – paper having iridescent and reflective properties

**Metallic ribbon** – ribbon having iridescent and reflective properties

**Monofilament thread** – a single untwisted synthetic filament (as of nylon)

**Motif** – a dominant idea or central theme; a single or repeated design or color

**Needle-nose pliers** – a small pincer for holding small objects or for bending and cutting wire

**Paint pen** – paint tubes often used for fabric painting, available at fabric, discount, and craft stores

**Parchment paper** – strong, tough, and often somewhat translucent paper

**Putty knife** – an implement with a broad flat metal blade used especially for applying putty and for scraping

**Raffia** – a fiber used for tying plants and making baskets and hats

**Rickrack** – a flat braid woven to form zigzags and used especially as trimming on clothing

**Round jewels** – small ball-shaped pieces of faceted glass or plastic used for ornamentation

**Running stitch** – a small even stitch running in and out of cloth

**Sequins** – small glittering objects or particles used for ornamentation

**Styrofoam** – a brand name for plastic foam; expanded plastic; lightweight cellular plastic commonly used in formed shapes such as round, wreath, rectangular, and cone shapes

**Tacky glue** – a sticky white glue that dries clear and can be used on fabric, silk, burlap, paper, decorations, and jewelry; especially designed for scrapcrafts or when gluing odd surfaces such as wood, metal, glass, ceramic, paper, china, Styrofoam, and most plastics

**Topiary** – training, cutting, or shaping trees or shrubs into odd or ornamental shapes

**Tracing paper** – a semi-transparent paper for tracing drawings

**Tulle** – a sheer often stiffened silk, rayon, or nylon net used chiefly for veils or ballet costumes

**Tussie mussie** – a paper or plastic bouquet holder found in the bridal section of crafts stores

**Varathane spray** – An oil-based varnish-type spray used to protect surfaces

**Votive candle** – a small squat candle

**Waffle cone** – a crisp cake of pancake batter baked in a waffle iron and shaped in a cone for ice cream

**Whipstitch** – a shallow overcasting stitch

**Wire-edge taffeta ribbon** – a crisp plain-woven lustrous fabric of various fibers made into a ribbon with tiny wire woven into the edges of the ribbon for pliability

# index

# index continued

# recipes

## Silly Popcorn Treats Recipe
*See project on page 16.*

- 18 cups popped popcorn
- 2 cups sugar
- 1 cup water
- ½ cup light-colored corn syrup
- 1 teaspoon vinegar
- ½ teaspoon salt
- 1 tablespoon vanilla
  Gummy worms, candy corn, and other Halloween candies

### Method
Remove all unpopped kernels from popped popcorn. Put popcorn in a greased 17×12×2-inch baking or roasting pan. Keep popcorn warm in a 300° oven while making syrup.

For syrup mixture, butter the sides of a heavy 2-quart saucepan. In saucepan combine sugar, water, corn syrup, vinegar, and salt. Cook and stir over medium-high heat till mixture boils, stirring to dissolve sugar (about 6 minutes). Clip a candy thermometer to side of pan. Reduce heat to medium; continue boiling at a moderate, steady rate, stirring occasionally, till thermometer registers 250°, hard-ball stage (about 20 minutes).

Remove saucepan from heat; remove thermometer. Stir in vanilla. Pour syrup mixture over the hot popcorn and stir gently to coat, adding candies. Cool till the popcorn mixture can be handled easily. With buttered hands, quickly shape the mixture into 2½-inch diameter balls. Wrap each popcorn ball in plastic wrap. Makes about 20 popcorn balls.

## Royal Frosting Recipe
*See project on page 87.*

- 3 eggs whites
- 1 6-ounce package powdered sugar, sifted
- 1 teaspoon vanilla
- ½ teaspoon cream of tartar

### Method
In a large bowl combine egg whites, powdered sugar, vanilla, and cream of tartar. Beat with an electric mixer on high speed for 7 to 10 minutes or until very stiff. Keep icing covered with plastic wrap at all times to prevent it from drying out. May be refrigerated overnight in tightly covered container; stir before using. Makes 3 cups.

## Gingerbread-Friends Garland Recipe
*See project on page 71.*

- ½ cup shortening
- ½ cup sugar
- 1 teaspoon baking powder
- 1 teaspoon ground ginger
- ½ teaspoon baking soda
- ½ teaspoon ground cinnamon
- ½ teaspoon ground cloves
- ½ cup molasses
- 1 egg
- 1 tablespoon vinegar
- 2½ cups all-purpose flour

### Method
In a mixing bowl beat shortening with an electric mixer on medium to high speed 30 seconds. Add sugar, baking powder, ginger, baking soda, cinnamon, and cloves. Beat till combined, scraping bowl. Beat in the molasses, egg, and vinegar till combined. Beat in as much of the flour as you can with the mixer. Stir in remaining flour. Divide dough in half. Cover and chill for 3 hours or till easy to handle.

Grease a cookie sheet; set aside. On a lightly floured surface, roll half of the dough at a time to ⅛-inch thick. Using a 1½-inch cookie cutter, cut into desired shapes. Place 1 inch apart on the prepared cookie sheet. Add holes at hands using a straw.

Bake in a 375° oven for 5 to 6 minutes or till edges are lightly browned. Cool on cookie sheet 1 minute. Transfer cookies to a wire rack and let cool. If desired, decorate cookies with icing and candies. Makes 36 to 48 cookies.

## photographers and designers:

**Photographers:**
King Au: Page 60
Hopkins Associates: Pages 57, 68, 184–185
John Kane: Pages 24, 46–47, 94, 98
Peter Krumhardt: Pages 10, 14, 16–17, 20, 22, 32–34, 56–57, 82–83, 84, 90, 92, 114
Scott Little: Pages 11, 25, 28–29, 35, 44–45, 78–79, 80, 82–83, 96–97, 110–111, 122–123, 124–125, 127, 164
Andy Lyons: Front cover and pages 8–9, 12–13, 21, 26–27, 30–31, 36–37, 38–39, 40–41, 42–43, 52–53, 54, 55, 58, 62–63, 64, 66–67, 71, 72–73, 74, 76–77, 87, 88–89, 91, 93, 95, 100–101, 102–103, 106–107, 108–109, 112–113, 116–117, 118, 120, 128–129, 134–135, 138–139, 140–141, 142, 143, 144–145, 146–147, 148–149, 151, 152–153, 154, 155, 156–157, 158–159, 160–161, 162–163, 165, 166, 168–169, 170, 171, 172–173, 174, 180, 186, 192–193, 194, 196–197, 198, 199, 200–201, 202–203, 204, 206, 207, 208, 210–211
Photo Styling: Carol Dahlstrom
Photo Styling Assistant: Donna Chesnut

**Designers:**
Susan Banker: Pages 12, 13, 22, 26–27, 38, 55, 56–57, 66, 84, 96–97, 120–121, 122–123, 142, 190, 204
Donna Chesnut: Pages 10, 16–17, 59, 64–65, 74, 78–79, 108–109, 140–141, 174, 207
Carol Dahlstrom: Pages 30–31, 32–34, 36, 52, 62–63, 72–73, 76–77, 82–83, 100, 112–113, 116–117, 127, 128–129, 134, 158–159, 160, 162–163, 168–169, 170, 171, 172, 184–185, 199, 208, 210–211
Marisa Dirks: Page 54
Phyllis Dobbs: Pages 58, 80, 118, 136, 143, 144, 151, 155, 166, 180, 191, 198
Phyllis Dunstan: Pages 8, 11, 14, 20, 25, 28, 42, 68, 106, 124, 146, 148, 152–153, 154, 165, 192–193, 194, 196–197, 206
Margaret Sindelar: Pages 88, 90–92, 102, 202
Karen Taylor: Pages 57, 87, 164, 186
Alice Wetzel: Pages 110, 138, 200